VULCA
ON THE
LINE

Brian Carlin

with

Geoff Supple
& others

iv

ISBN: 9781796744712
Imprint: Independently published by Brian Carlin

Published by Brian Carlin

VULCAN ON THE LINE

Other books by Brian Carlin

Boy Entrant

Kestrel Squadron

Dedicated to the friends and colleagues with whom I served on Flight Line Squadron, RAF Waddington, when we were members of the Vulcan ground crews. Also to our wives and families who suffered when calls to duty meant being separated from their loved ones.

TABLE OF CONTENTS

Preface

Those of us who came of age, or were already of age, in the 1950s and 1960s during the so-called Cold War lived under the constant threat of nuclear annihilation at the hands of the USSR. To counter the threat, the Western Powers developed a 'Nuclear Deterrent', which promised Mutually Assured Destruction (MAD) should the Russians precipitate a nuclear 'first-strike' against any country in the West. Initially, Britain's contribution to the Nuclear Deterrent took the form of the nuclear weapons-capable V-Bomber fleet; the Vulcan, Victor and Valiant aircraft.

The V-Bombers, originally painted overall in bright white 'anti-flash' livery, were designed as high altitude bombers that carried no defensive armament, but relied purely on their ability to fly at a very high altitude for protection from ground attacks. Later, when the perceived enemy's capabilities improved to an extent that high altitude was no longer an effective defence, the V-bombers were re-deployed in a low-level attack role. As a result, the livery on the upper surface of the aircraft was changed to a camouflage while the lower surface retained its anti-flash coating.

Throughout all of this, the aircrews constantly trained to carry their deadly cargoes to the heart of the enemy territory. Many books have been written on this topic. Behind the scenes, as it were, the ground crews and maintenance personnel supported the nuclear deterrent effort, but little, if anything, has been written about their role. In a modest way, this book aims to correct that discrepancy and is written from the point of view of someone who served as a member of the Vulcan ground crews together with contributions from others in the same or in supportive roles.

Chapter 1: A Dream Posting

It was the best of times, it was the worst of times, to shamelessly parrot Charles Dickens' famous opening line; it was the early 1960s.

The best was that the British aviation industry was, arguably, at its peak; Avro, Handley Page, and Vickers had all produced their versions of the V-bombers the Vulcan, the Victor and the Valiant. The sleek, deadly, English Electric Lightning was in service, the world's first VSTOL fighter was well along in its development and an evaluation version of the P1127 would soon enter service as the Kestrel. Following along behind these were the revolutionary but ill-fated TSR2 and supersonic VSTOL P1154.

The worst was that we were in the middle of the Cold War. Our V-bombers were poised to deliver "instant sunshine" to targets in the Soviet Union, should it attempt a 'first strike' on any NATO member's country. Russian Bears, constantly probing our defences, were intercepted by QRA Lightnings that rose like silvery trout from the sea of overcast cloud that frequently covered our home islands.

As members of the RAF, we all played our part and at a personal level, as a highly-trained electrical technician, my crucial role in the defence of the Realm was to service and maintain a Flight of De Havilland Chipmunks. These small, piston-engine training aircraft possessed an electrical system hardly more sophisticated than that of a 1960s era Ford Prefect. But thankfully, a higher calling awaited when the RAF saw fit to pluck me out of a cosy little relationship with the 'Chippy' and insert me into a totally different environment, centred on the then state-of-the-art Vulcan Mk B2. Finally, *finally*, I was now going to be working on 'real' aircraft. I had spent four years servicing the Dinky toys operated by the Royal Air Force College Cranwell, where I had been stationed since leaving Boy Entrant training. Not only that, but it came with a posting that could only have been a gift from Heaven. Let me back up a little to explain all of that.

Since arriving at Cranwell in 1958 as an Electrical Mechanic (qualified to change batteries, light bulbs and not much else), I had worked mostly on Vampires. Then, after returning from my Electrical Fitter's course in 1960 with the exalted rank of Junior Technician and armed to the teeth with cutting edge knowledge, I was ready for much more technically challenging electrical work that would exercise my new-found skills. The Electrical Engineering Officer had other ideas, however. He decided that my best contribution to the smooth running of the College's mission would be for me to assume the role of senior electrician on the College Chipmunk Flight.

The flight consisted of nine or ten De Havilland Chipmunks operating from a grass airfield, known as the North Airfield, with the purpose of providing flying familiarization to first-year Cranwell cadets before they started serious pilot training in their second year. The maintenance staff consisted of one Sergeant, two corporals and two representatives of each aircraft trade applicable to the Chipmunk – Engine, Airframe, Electrical and Radio, typically a mechanic and technician for each trade. It was an easy life on the Flight. There was no night flying, we finished at a civilized time each day and flying was cancelled if there was the slightest hint of fog or a strong breeze. In between, there were plenty of opportunities to go flying because desk-bound pilots on "ground tours" made use of the Chipmunks to put in the minimum number of flying hours they needed to qualify for flying pay.

One day, in April of 1962, after about two years on the Chipmunk Flight, I was called into the Flight office to take a phone call from the Station Orderly Room. It was from a corporal with whom I was acquainted and considered a friend, based on our mutual Irish origin. He started the conversation by telling me that an overseas posting had come through for me. He wasn't immediately forthcoming on where I was to be posted, but instead asked if I liked cigars. This puzzled me because I couldn't see any connection between cigars and an overseas posting. He then told me it was to America.

Author Brian Carlin posing in one of the RAF College Cranwell Chipmunks.

To be more precise, my posting was to Eglin Air Force Base in Florida. I would be taking part in the trials of the Douglas Skybolt air-launched nuclear missile, which the British government had purchased from the United States to be carried on our Vulcan bombers. However, the actual move to Eglin was some months away. There was much preparation needed, and part of my new job was to assist in some of those preparations. To this end, I was directed to report to the Electronics Centre at RAF Coningsby, where I would join a team of other Electrical Fitters. Our task was to build electrical test consoles for the planned Electrical Servicing Bay at Eglin, where electrical components periodically removed from the Vulcans would be serviced.

Two gifts in one package; a posting to America was the icing on the cake and to be working on Vulcans had to be the cherry. I had long enjoyed seeing the Vulcans from the A15 Sleaford to Lincoln road, while regularly travelling to and from Lincoln during my time at Cranwell. The road passed very close to the threshold of the main Waddington runway and one or more Vulcans were usually parked on the Bravo dispersal when I passed, (although I didn't know it was

Bravo at the time). The sight of the large aircraft sitting on the dispersal in their white anti-flash livery was a joy to see and if timing was on my side, the traffic light on the A15, just short of the runway, would turn to red. That's when I was in for the even bigger treat of seeing a Vulcan come in to land.

At first, looking out over the flat expanse of Lincolnshire countryside, the distant aircraft's position would be marked by the tell-tale, dark, smoky trail of the jet exhausts. Then, as it drew nearer, the shape could be better discerned, emphasised by the black legs legs and wheels of the lowered landing gear. Finally, the elegant delta would glide past in a nose-up configuration, seemingly just in front of the waiting traffic, its four Olympus engines whistling at idling revolutions as it gracefully descended to execute a touchdown on the runway, rearing up into the Vulcan's hallmark planform to act as a giant air brake after twin puffs of smoke marked the moment that the main wheels made contact with the tarmac. Soon after that, its brake parachute would billow for a time, until released near the far end of the runway. The traffic lights would then turn green and the road journey resumed.

It was sights such as this that made me envious of those who were stationed at Waddington and associated with operational aircraft, instead of being part of the glorified flying club that was Cranwell.

In the meantime, as well as being detached to Coningsby, I was instructed to fill out a questionnaire for "positive vetting, top". This was because the Skybolt Trial was classified as top secret, so it was necessary for my background to be checked so that I could be granted the appropriate security clearance. There were some consequences attached to this, one of which I did not learn about until many years later. The questionnaire required me to provide names of people that I knew well who could provide references. One of these was Richard Butterworth, my good friend from my Boy Entrant training days, who had also been posted to Cranwell with me, so our friendship had continued up until I left Cranwell on this posting. Many years later, we met up again at our Entry's reunion. At this re-acquaintance, he quickly brought up the subject of the vetting and went on to say that a member of the Special Investigative Branch (SIB) of the RAF police interviewed him to ask questions about our friendship. One of the questions asked was whether or not our friendship was of a homosexual nature. After 50 years, Richard was still annoyed about that question and let me know in no uncertain manner. There was another consequence of the vetting process that surprised and shook me, but more about that later.

Vulcan approaching the runway at Waddington in the landing configuration.
Photo courtesy of Eric Bickley-Faux from his father Barry Bickley's collection

Chapter 2: Paxolin and Courses

Coningsby wasn't very far from Cranwell, so I was able to get there a few days later thanks to my then girlfriend Marion, who drove me there in her Austin Mini. After going through the normal 'arrival' formalities, I reported to the lead corporal in charge of our efforts. We spent the next few weeks sawing and filing 'Paxolin' sheets to make holes for electrical meters, switches, indicator lights and various other components that would make up the test boards. These, then were to be packed up for shipment to Eglin at some future date. It was boring work and a bit of a letdown after the initial excitement of getting the 'America' posting. To make matters worse, I did not get on too well with the lead corporal, (I'll call him Corporal X). He was extremely critical of my work and just made that part of the experience miserable. He apparently knew Squadron Leader Lawson, the Skybolt Trials Engineering Officer, and sucked up to him at every opportunity by bringing up the subject of some kind of test equipment that he, Corporal X, had "invented" when they were both at RAF Scampton.

Thankfully, the work at Coningsby was interrupted seven weeks later, when four of us on the team were sent on a 6-week Vulcan-Victor electrical course to RAF Melksham, (Number 12 School of Technical Training), where I had previously undergone my Fitter's Course. We four had not previously worked on Vulcans, so it was rightly felt that we should be educated on the sophisticated electrical system with which the Mark 2 Vulcans and Victors were equipped, and which was a quantum leap ahead of any of the aircraft electrical systems I had been trained on or had experienced up to that point.

The Mk B2 V-bombers, Vulcan and Victor, were equipped with a 200 Volt AC, 400 Hz electrical system, which was a major departure from the traditional low voltage 28 Volt DC system with which most RAF aircraft had been equipped up to that time. Grasping the electrical concepts used in this system was extremely challenging to all of us taking the course. Even then, the instructor did everything possible to make it easier for us to understand. The trouble was, speaking for myself, I had not been educated to the level necessary to fully understand the mathematics related to the system, which involved vector analysis and trigonometric functions. I suspect this was also true for most of the others. The instructor did a great job of explaining, by working around the mathematics. In later years, when I studied for my Higher National Certificate in electrical engineering, it became apparent to me what hoops he had had to jump through to simplify the information for us.

Thanks to our patient and knowledgeable instructor, we all passed the course, which ended in the middle of the first week of July 1962. Then, it was back to Coningsby again for continuation of the test boards, culminating in us packing them up in crates and labelling them for shipment under the code name, 'Home Noisy'. This lasted for a few weeks, but then we electricians were sent to the Avro factory at Woodford to be given some specialized instruction on the Vulcans that were currently being built specifically for the Skybolt trials. These aircraft, two of which were on the factory floor during our time there, had specially strengthened hard points to carry a Skybolt missile under both the port and starboard wings. It also had uprated Olympus engines that provided considerably greater thrust than the B2 Vulcans currently in service. In addition, they had been fitted with red rotating reflector style anti-collision lights to conform to the American Federal Aviation Administration (FAA) regulations, instead of the then-current three white on-and-off flashing white lights featured on the in-service Vulcans (B1s, B1As and B2s).

An interesting fact about these particular aircraft is that toward the end of their lives, they were selected to carry anti-radiation missiles for suppression of Argentinian radar installations during the Falklands war. The selection was based purely on the Skybolt hard points from which purpose-built pylons were attached to carry the anti- radiation missiles and the more powerful Olympus 301 engines that were needed to propel the all up weight of a full fuel load and heavy missiles. But, I digress.

For the duration of the course, we were billeted at a former military hospital, possibly the former Baguley Emergency Medical Services Hospital, which was then almost closed down and existed only as a transit type of location to billet personnel such as us. The permanent staff consisted of only a few individuals and the atmosphere was decidedly informal. For instance, the cook prepared our meals to order instead of the usual take it or leave it fare in normal RAF airmen's messes. A RAF bus picked us up in the morning for the long

Vulcan B2 carrying two dummy Skybolt missiles on pylons attached to special strong points built into the wings of the aircraft earrmarked for the Skybolt trials. Later, these same strong points came in handy for carrying Shrike missiles during the Falklands campaign.

Photo from www.PPrune.org..."did you fly the vulcan?"thread.

trip to the Avro factory and dropped us off there again in the evening.

On the course, we were joined by the other electricians assigned to Skybolt. These individuals were already serving on B2 Vulcans and were therefore well acquainted with the aircraft's complex electrical system, which is why we had not met them previously at the

Vulcan/Victor course at RAF Melksam. One of these was Corporal Gerry Gibson. He and I hit it off right away, which was a blessing, considering the strained relationship I was suffering with the Coningsby crew. Gerry was stationed on 230 Operational Conversion Unit (OCU) at RAF Finningley. Possibly, Gerry put in a good word for me with Squadron Leader Lawson because, when the Avro course ended, I was detached to 230 OCU at Finningley for on-the-job training under Gerry's supervision and mentorship. I arrived at Finningley, near Doncaster, Yorkshire, on 3rd of September 1962.

At Finningley, my world changed for the better. Gerry Gibson was the complete opposite of Corporal X at Coningsby and treated me as one of his mates. My other colleagues were equally great to work with, J/T Pete Thompson and Jim Connolly, a friendly acquaintance from my Boy Entrant training days. Jim had been in the 28th Entry, one entry ahead of me at St Athan.

Working on the Vulcans, under Gerry's supervision was satisfying, especially as my practical knowledge of the aircraft increased and I was able to prove to myself and others that I could contribute. There are times in our lives when we suddenly become aware that we have crossed a certain threshold of capability and this happened to me one day, with regard to the Vulcan. It was while checking something in the crew cabin of one particular aircraft

230 OCU badge

that I overheard an Air Radar Chief Technician swearing and cursing in the rear crew cabin because he was having trouble bringing the Electronic Counter Measures (ECM) cooling system on line. He kept trying, while vehemently exclaiming his frustration, but without success – the cooling system doll's eye indicator just flicked back to white every time he released the spring-loaded switch. Remembering something from my Woodford training course, I noticed that although electrical power was being applied to the Vulcan from a ground power unit, the 24 volt battery was not switched on, which meant that an electrical interlock in the ECM cooling system was disabled. Descending from the flight deck, I went over to the AEO's (Air Electronics Operator) position and flicked the battery switch to "on" and then suggested that he try starting the cooling system again. This time the cooling system doll's eye stayed black. The Chief Tech thanked me profusely and praised me to high heaven, as though I were some kind of genius. I felt a flush of pride along with the realization that, although it was a small thing, somehow I had 'made it' as a Vulcan electrical technician. I also felt proud that I was no longer twiddling my thumbs playing funfair attendant on the Chipmunk Flight at Cranwell, but doing something useful as a small part of Britain's Nuclear Deterrent – the V-bomber force. Little did I know that the deadly role of the V-bomber force would be demonstrated very realistically shortly after my arrival at Finningley.

At one point, Squadron Leader Lawson visited the electrical section and in front of me, cautioned Gerry to keep and eye on me and not let me slack off or something to that effect. It was obvious that Corporal X from Coningsby had been putting words in his ear about me. Gerry, to his credit and to my great joy, replied that I was doing a fine job. I certainly hoped that I would be working with Gerry when we got to Eglin AFB and not Corporal X. Socially it was also a very satisfying situation because Pete Thompson also befriended me. Gerry, who lived in married quarters, often came to our barrack room on Saturday mornings to roust us out of bed so that we three could go into Doncaster and have a few pints of beer at one of the many pubs in the city.

Just as a side note; Vulcan XH558, which gained fame many years later as the last airworthy Vulcan was also the first Mk B2 to be delivered to the RAF as a replacement for the Mks B1 and B1A. Since 230 OCU was the unit that converted aircrew to the Vulcan, it was to the OCU that XH558 was delivered on the 1st of July 1960 while the OCU was based at RAF Waddington, although it moved to RAF Finningley very soon afterwards. During my service with 230 OCU, I worked on all of six or so of the Unit's Mk B2 aircraft, so without a doubt I can confidentially state that XH558 was one of those to which I rendered loving care.

Chapter 3: The Cuban Missile Crisis

Most of those stationed at Finningley and the other V-bomber stations were well drilled when it came to 'alert' conditions. Two or three times a week, without fail, aircraft and crews on QRA (Quick Reaction Alert) were brought to the state of 5-minute readiness when a loud klaxon sound blared from Tannoys throughout the station, followed by the announcement, "Exercise Edom! Exercise Edom! Readiness state, zero five". The message, broadcast directly from Bomber Command HQ at High Wycombe, sent the airmen assigned to the QRA Vulcans scrambling hastily from the mess hall, leaving unfinished meals on the table, as they raced back to the QRA dispersal to man the nuclear-armed aircraft. Then there were the periodic alerts, Exercise Mick or an Exercise Mickey Finn, either of which brought the entire station to 15-minute readiness. These two exercises meant that everyone had to report to their place of duty immediately. As with the QRA alerts, the Tannoy system unexpectedly began broadcasting the loud klaxon sound, followed by the Bomber Controller's announcement, declaring the specific exercise code name. Service Police roamed the married patch in Land Rovers, , broadcasting the klaxon through loudspeakers. There was even a system in place for rapidly contacting those who lived off the station by phoning a designated living-out NCO, who would then either phone three or four other individuals to notify them, or physically go to their residences to inform them in person.

The Mick exercise involved bringing every aircraft possible to a state of serviceability, even those in the hangar undergoing minor and major second line servicing. The exercise was fulfilled when the aircraft were armed with dummy weapons and brought to 15-readiness. Inevitably, one or maybe two aircraft could not be generated, in which case they became candidates to be cannibalized for the serviceable parts needed to bring the recoverable aircraft up to operational readiness.

Everyone associated with aircraft maintenance and support knew very well to bring a small kit containing toiletries and a few changes of clothing when a Mick alert went off. This was because it was well known that a 'Mick' could very well evolve into a 'Mickey

Finn', which then meant that all operationally-ready aircraft would be dispersed to non-bomber stations throughout the length and breadth of the land, to minimize the risk of them being taken out by an enemy first-strike on their home bases. When a Mickey Finn was called, in the first instance, all of the activities associated with a Mick would be performed, and then each aircraft would be dispersed as it reached operational readiness. Dispersal of the V-force aircraft was the standard operating procedure for an alert condition, based on the assumption that any crisis would be preceded by a deteriorating state of international relations, giving ample warning of an impending nuclear exchange. At least that was the military plan, but as we shall learn, plans can be ditched when politicians are involved.

All of this, I learned later on, but my first experience of an 'Alert' turned out to be the real thing. It has gone down in the history books as The Cuban Missile Crisis.

The trigger that kicked off that infamous incident occurred when American reconnaissance aircraft photographed Russian nuclear missile sites being constructed on the island nation of Cuba and then, a few days later, ships laden with Russian missiles were seen heading towards Cuba. Russia refused to turn the ships around and so, on Friday, 26th of October, the Americans increased the USAF Strategic Air Command to alert level 'Defcon 2': just one notch below the highest level that anticipates an imminent attack. The ratcheting up of the American war readiness precipitated the ensuing 'Mexican Standoff' between President John F. Kennedy and Russian Premier Nikita Khrushchev.

The British Government's official line during the crisis was one of non-involvement. Prime Minister Harold Macmillan blandly announced on the BBC that the fuss was all between the Americans and Russians and that Britain was taking no special action in the crisis. The British public swallowed this, hook line and sinker, but it was a bold-faced lie that was far removed from the truth because, when the Americans went to Defcon 2, RAF Bomber Command also brought the V-bomber squadrons, including 230 OCU, to 15-minute readiness state: the British equivalent of Defcon 2.

As was the usual case, the klaxon blared from the Tannoy to notify all within earshot of the alert condition, but this time it was not preceded by the word 'exercise'. Instead, during the broadcast, the Bomber Controller specifically stated several times that "this is not an exercise". Nevertheless, the well-practised 'Exercise Mick' procedures went into full swing, ordering all personnel to their places of duty. A Mick involved just about everyone on a bomber station. Aircraft servicing personnel, of course, commenced 'generating' the aircraft, but others had their roles to play; the service police increased the already tight security, the MT section mobilized for the anticipated dispersal, Stores prepared for the task of issuing aircraft service parts or for bringing them from other stations on a VOG (V-bomber on the ground) priority. Even the catering staff made ready to ship out with dispersed crews to man field kitchens at the dispersal airfields, at which the detached contingents were expected to be self-sufficient. Transport Command also got involved by making their Hercules aircraft immediately available to whisk ground crews and equipment to far-flung dispersal airfields.

As I mentioned earlier, most people in the V-force knew what to do when an alert was declared, but having been at Finningley for just a couple of months, this was my first experience of the whole station going to operational readiness. And wasn't it just my fantastic luck that instead of it being just an exercise, this was the real thing!

On the first day, I worked with the others to help bring all 230 OCU aircraft up to full serviceability, at the same time being somewhat awestruck at seeing armourers and riggers winching real nuclear weapons up into the Vulcan bomb bays. The nukes were massive, each filling the entire bomb bay of a Vulcan. They were not as one might imagine – although equipped with fins at the rear end, the front end had a peculiar flattened appearance where one would have expected to see a rounded nose. Their colour was a dull green on a textured-like surface, which hinted at an outer covering of some type, possibly fibreglass. See (http://en.wikipedia.org/wiki/Yellow_Sun).).

A Yellow Sun free-fall nuclear bomb on display at the RAF Museum, Cosford.
The weapon that I observed in a Vulcan bomb bay did not have the polished
exterior shown here

Photo: By Nabokov at English Wikipedia, CC BY-SA 3.0,
https://commons.wikimedia.org/w/index.php?curid=17668771

We all knew that the flap had something to do the Cuban missile situation, but in typical service fashion, no one was telling us anything. That was probably because our superiors didn't know either and were just following orders. By the end of the first day, most aircraft had been 'recovered', the first four of which were towed to the ORP – the Operational Readiness Platform – a concrete apron adjoining the left-hand side of the runway at its extreme end. The Vulcans parked on the ORP were angled towards the runway, to facilitate a rapid takeoff. Very soon, I joined them as a member of one of the starter ground crews.

For the duration of the alert, we were to be housed in several mobile units that were configured as sleeping accommodation, which had been brought to the ORP some time earlier. Most of these 'caravans' were divided into individual sleeping compartments containing bunk beds. There was an additional mobile unit that was configured as an office cum crew-room.

A squadron of Vulcans on the ORP, ready to scramble.
Photo courtesy of Eric Bickley-Faux from his father Barry Bickley's collection

On that first day, as was typical in my service days, when something out of the ordinary disturbed the normal routine, all was total chaos. Getting meals was one of the problems, since none of us were able or permitted to go to the mess, even though we didn't have the means anyway, being stuck at the end of the runway. Eventually, sandwiches and urns of tea were brought out from the mess. The sandwiches were far from appetising and after taking a few bites to ward off the pangs of hunger, most of us didn't indulge ourselves too heartily.

By the second day, some semblance of order had asserted itself and transport was laid on to take us to the mess in small groups, leaving a sufficient number of ground crew at the ORP to man the aircraft should the readiness level be increased. During this time, some of us were able to visit the TV room in the NAAFI to watch the evening news, with the hope of finding out what was going on. I recall seeing Mr. Macmillan either being interviewed or making a speech, but clearly remember that he assured viewers not to be alarmed because Britain was taking no action in regard to the crisis. This prompted hoots of derision from those of us watching the television.

Back at the ORP, the question on everyone's mind was "Why aren't we being dispersed, in keeping with the frequently practised strategy?" Having all of the V-Force's bombers concentrated at their home bases made them (and us) sitting ducks for a first strike by the Russians. Many years later, we learned that Prime Minister Macmillan had deliberately ordered the Air Chiefs not to disperse the aircraft in order not to alert the Russians that we had gone to a high state of readiness. It also later came to light, however, that the Russians knew very well what was going on, and actually planned for their first strikes to be directed at Britain, because we were the more immediate threat, being nearer to Moscow than America's Strategic Air Command bombers. As alluded to earlier, military strategies are useless when politicians are allowed to pull the strings.

We remained at 15-minute readiness all through Friday, but on Saturday the Tannoy at the ORP crackled to life with the announcement, "This is the Bomber Controller, readiness condition zero five, I repeat readiness condition zero five."

Chairs were knocked aside as we tumbled out of the crew room and ran to our assigned Vulcans in response to the newly announced 5-minutes readiness condition. The Crew Chief was already there; he had opened the aircraft entrance hatch and then lowered the access ladder, ready for the crew to climb up inside. Standing alongside our designated stations, we now awaited the arrival of the aircrew. Electrical power, 28 volts DC and 200 volts AC was already connected to the aircraft as a condition of the prior 15-minute readiness state.

Moments later, four crew coaches came tearing along the taxiway heading in our direction, one behind the other. On reaching the ORP, they split up and each made for an individual aircraft, screeching to a halt alongside the nose section. At the Vulcan where I was stationed, the folding doors of the coach were thrown open by a grim-faced aircrew member, who then sprinted for the entrance hatch, followed by his four other crew members.

It needs to be mentioned that these were seasoned aircrew from RAF Waddington. With the exception of instructors, the 230 OCU aircrew were all trainees converting from other aircraft types to the Vulcan. Their familiarity with this aircraft was basic; they therefore did not have the necessary experience or knowledge to be sent on a bombing mission of this nature.

The men quickly ascended into the bowels of the Vulcan crew compartment and shortly afterwards, the Air Electronics Officer started the 'Rover' auxiliary power unit (APU) from his position on the port side of the crew compartment. The APU provided on-board electrical power that now made the ground power redundant, so the power cables could be removed and dragged out of the way. This was all in anticipation of the readiness state being ratcheted up to the next level, which would have been 'zero two' – start engines. Should that happen, all four engines would be started simultaneously by using compressed air reservoirs located in the bomb bay. At that point, we would be moments away from launching the aircraft on a one way trip to Russia.

The Crew Chief signalled for the groundcrew manning the external 28 volt and 200 volt ground power cables to pull them out of the sockets that connected the electrical power to the aircraft. The Vulcan was now independent of ground power and capable of starting its own engines from the on-board compressed air. Meanwhile, those of us standing by the chocks watched the Crew Chief's every move, since an engine start would have also been accompanied by the 'chocks away' hand signal. The moment was tense, but all thoughts of the seriousness of the situation were distant as we concentrated on doing our jobs. The question of what would happen afterwards, should the Vulcans take off, was hardly dwelled upon. In fact, no one had told us what we should do afterwards. As a 22-year old, I was imbued with the strong sense of immortality common to most young people and had no doubts about coming through whatever happened unscathed. In retrospect, I wonder what actually would have happened, and just hoped that there was some kind of contingency plan to get everyone remaining behind into some form of shelter, perhaps the hardened bunkers where the nuclear weapons had, until very recently, been stored. Although an attack on the station after the Vulcans had departed would have been futile from the Russian strategic point of view, it was a very real possibility in the fog of war. As for the Vulcans: the aircrew had standing orders that after delivering their weapons on their target, they were on their own. Chances were that there would be no base to return to, so they should seek a safe haven wherever they could find it.

We stood underneath the Vulcan for what seemed an eternity and then suddenly the Crew Chief indicated that ground power should be restored. The men responsible for the cables quickly plugged them back in and opened the throttle on the Ground Power Unit's diesel engine, which revved up dramatically, before quickly levelling off at its automatically governed speed. When that happened, within a matter of seconds, one of the men pushed the 'on' switches that applied both types electrical power to the aircraft. Soon the Vulcan crew door unlatched and swung downwards in a smooth glide, as the Crew Chief came aft from his position by the nose wheel to lift the lower part of the access ladder down from its stowage and lock it in position in readiness for the crew to dismount. Relief swept visibly over all of us – we were back to 15-minute readiness, at least for now. No one there was in any position to predict if and when the alert state would be raised again.

As it happened, the crisis fever had peaked in those few minutes and would never reach that level in anger again. Khrushchev backed down and ordered the ships carrying the missiles to turn around and head back to the Baltic. In the following days, he agreed to dismantle the missile sites on Cuba, but in return, received an assurance from Kennedy that the American missile sites in Turkey would also be dismantled. This is what Russia wanted all along; it was the presence of US missiles in Turkey, virtually in Russia's backyard, that had prompted Khrushchev to start building his tit-for-tat sites in Cuba in the first place.

All returned to normal at Finningley. It took another day or two to return the Vulcans to their normal peacetime condition, but as a young man, I was just glad to be able to get off camp again and enjoy the delights of nearby Doncaster. All it had amounted to was a lost weekend. Looking back, it seems more frightening that we all came so close to being wiped out in a nuclear holocaust, especially so when the majority of people in the British Isles would not have had the slightest inkling of what was about to hit them until the bombs and ballistic missiles came raining in. But by then, it wouldn't have mattered.

Postscript

Some readers may get a feeling of *déjà vu* in that they have read the foregoing chapter elsewhere in the past and that is absolutely possible. Originally, I wrote it for publication as an article in the RAF Boy Entrants Association (RAFBEA) newsletter in May 2010, which appeared in the newsletter later that year. But it doesn't end there.

Early in December 2014, I received an email sent on behalf of the London Bureau Chief of the *Asahi Shimbun*, Mr. Toshiya Umehara. (The *Asahi Shimbun* is a Japanese newspaper with a large, worldwide circulation). The email went on to say that Mr. Umehara had been very interested in my *Boy Entrant* book and in particular my experiences during the Cuban Missile Crisis, including the role played by the Vulcan bombers and that he was willing to fly out from London to San Diego for the interview. A few days later, we met for the interview in a San Diego hotel conference room that he had reserved for that purpose.

During the interview, we went over the content of the article that had appeared in the RAFBEA newsletter and although he asked a few questions, I had very little else that I could add. Umehara took a few headshot photographs of me and then, after a light lunch together, he departed to catch the next plane back to London. I couldn't believe that he had flown all that way for such a brief interview.

During our lunch, however, when conversation was a little more relaxed, I inquired as to how he had found me. It transpired that he first came across my account of the Cuban Missile Crisis in *Britain On The Brink,* a book by Jim Wilson. He then dug around on the Internet until he found my *Boy Entrant* book and from there my email address. Later, Out of curiosity, I obtained a copy of *Britain On The Brink* and, sure enough, discovered that it regurgitated a large chunk of my RAFBEA article verbatim in chapter 14 of the book. On parting, Mr. Umehara assured me that he would send me a copy of his article, which was supposed to appear in the *Asahi Shimbun* the following Sunday. One year later, however, a copy of the article had yet to show up, so I phoned the newspaper's London bureau and spoke with Mr. Umehara's assistant – the Englishman who had originally communicated with me by email. He very kindly sent me a pdf copy of the article but apologized that it was in Japanese and that no English translation existed. My skill at reading Japanese is on a par with my skill for reading Ancient Sumerian Cuneiform; zero in other words. However, the assistant suggested that perhaps I could find a Japanese person willing to translate it.

Considerable time passed before I was eventually able to obtain a translation. It turned out that the wily Umehara had simply condensed my article, mangling a few words, such as 'Vulcan' and 'Finningley', in the process. It then became obvious why the interview was so short – he just wanted the cover of being able to say that he had obtained his information by interviewing me and not by cribbing from my article. Well, at least I got a free lunch out of it!

Chapter 4: The name's Bond; James Bond...

Life soon settled back to normal after the Cuban Missile Crisis had been defused and it was just a memory several days later when I was summoned to the SHQ Orderly Room where a clerk handed me a buff coloured envelope bearing the familiar OHMS initials – shorthand for 'On Her Majesty's Service'. Inside, a letter under the official Air Ministry letterhead contained some very peculiar instructions together with a railway warrant for a return ticket to London. My instructions were to travel to London on a certain date, a few days hence. On arrival in London, I was to make my way to Acton Town Hall and report at a certain time to a certain Squadron Leader in a department named Security Services. The instructions also emphasised that I was not to wear my uniform, but to travel there in civilian clothes. I had never heard of Security Services before, but the name sounded ominous. Nor have I since, but I now suspect that it was a branch of the feared SIB – the RAF Special Investigation Branch.

Back at the hangar, I told Gerry Gibson and Pete Thompson about this strange directive. We had all recently seen the new and first of the series of James Bond films, *Dr. No*, so the apparently secretive circumstances surrounding my trip took on an even more sinister cloak and dagger aspect. Remember, security around the V-bombers during the Cold War was very tight, so a department that incorporated the word 'Security' in its name had the tendency to induce a little anxiety. When I told the others, Pete laughed and said it was probably because I was Irish. He might have thought it was funny, but it seemed a reasonable explanation to me and one that caused me some anxiety. I didn't want to be removed from the trials on the basis of my origins.

On the appointed day, I caught a train to London. At least Doncaster was on the main line to Kings Cross, so the trip didn't take too long. After taking the Underground to Acton, which is within the London metropolitan area, I arrived in the vicinity of the town hall about an hour too early for my appointment. That gave me a little extra time to reconnoitre the area to see where I was supposed to go. Having done that, I then went into a small nearby café for something to eat and to while away the remaining time over a cup of tea.

Shortly before the time for my appointment, I went into the town hall and in the lobby, was directed to a security post at the entrance to one wing of the building. The post was guarded by a black-uniformed Air Ministry constable. Walking over to him, I presented him with the letter that had summoned me there together with my RAF identity card, both of which he examined closely. He then told me to wait while he made a telephone call. What seemed like ages, but probably was very quickly, a uniformed RAF corporal arrived at the guard's post and bade me to come with him. After a short walk along some corridors, we arrived at an office that was obviously being used as an orderly room. The corporal indicated a comfortable armchair against a wall near his desk and gestured for me to sit there while telling me to wait until the Squadron Leader was ready to see me.

While I waited, an elderly gentleman came into the office. He had the appearance of a college professor, dressed in baggy trousers and a well worn, tweedy sports jacket complete with leather patches at the elbows. He seemed a kindly, jovial sort and joked with both the corporal and me. After he left the office with a cheery "goodbye," the corporal smiled and commented, "What do you think of that for an AVM?"

He, of course, meant an Air Vice Marshal – an exalted being who dwelled in the heady, rarefied air of the upper ranks of the Royal Air Force. The only other times that I had occasion to see an AVM was on the parade ground during ceremonial parades when such high-ranking officers inspected us lesser mortals in the ranks and then took the salute during our march-past. In those circumstances, they were always dressed in full regalia, complete with ceremonial sword and hat laden with 'scrambled egg' on its visor and frequently with a Knight's Cross of some Chivalrous Order or other around their neck. Never in my life did I expect to meet one of them wearing a scruffy sports jacket with patched up elbows.

Eventually, the corporal answered a phone call and then gave me a look that indicated my hour had come. He then escorted me to an office door on which he politely knocked. A man's voice on the other side said to come in, at which the corporal twisted the door knob to open the door a slight way, then stepped aside and motioned me to proceed into the office. On fully opening the door, I found myself in a roomy office where, behind a desk sat a well-dressed man in a civilian suit. He motioned me to sit in a chair on the opposite side of his desk and then introduced himself as the Squadron Leader with whom I had the appointment. He was friendly and tried to put me at ease.

"I suppose you know why you're here?" he said.

The question took me by surprise. It was my expectation to be told why I was there and not to participate in some guessing game. Influenced by my workmates back at Finningley, I was convinced that my national origin was the sole reason for being in this situation. I was in dread of being taken off the Skybolt trials because of it. "Is it because I'm Irish?" I ventured nervously.

If his question was unexpected, his reaction was even more so. He let out a loud laugh and then, with a smile, said, "No, your nationality isn't the reason." He paused for effect and then continued, "You've been writing letters haven't you? Telling people where you're going and what you're going to be doing."

I thought back to a letter I had written to my best pal from Cranwell, Johnny Leighton, who was now stationed overseas in Aden. In the letter, I had definitely blabbed about going to Eglin AFB and about the Skybolt.

"Yes, I wrote about it to a friend in Aden." I replied.

"Ah," he said, "so that's another one!"

The Squadron Leader then went on to lecture me at length on the need for security because the trials were top secret while I sat facing him across his desk, feeling mortified.

Chapter 5: Learning the Ropes

On 230 OCU, as on other V-Force squadrons, we worked alternate weeks of day shift and night shift. This aspect of the work I found to be stressful after my cushy life at Cranwell and it took quite a bit of getting used to. Worst was how the switch backwards and forwards played havoc with the digestive system. Eating the main meal of the day at 9 pm was something I never got used to, even though it was to be my lot for several years to come.

Sometimes, we would sit in a Vulcan and be towed to a remote part of the airfield, known as Bawtry, because it was near the village of the same name. That's where engine runs were carried out for a variety of reasons. Our job was to bring the electrical alternators on line to provide the necessary power. Often, we would also be testing for snags on the power generation equipment itself, or calibrating it. Because this sometimes happened late in the evening, the guardroom would receive complaints telephoned in by irate residents of Bawtry and the surrounding area whose evenings were interrupted by the powerful howl of the Vulcan's Olympus engines. Unfortunately for them, it was necessary to operate an engine at full power during certain parts of the engine run. When that happened, the whole aircraft lurched forward and went nose down in a violent motion, straining against the brakes and chocks. Sitting in the AEO's seat, I could feel the nose section dipping down in reaction to the powerful thrust and then, when the throttle was pulled back, it sprang back up to its level position. Nowadays, spectators love to hear the "mating call" of the B2 – the nickname we gave to the howl – but they probably wouldn't have appreciated it either if they were enjoying an otherwise relaxing evening watching the telly or, even worse, trying to get to sleep.

As one of the perks of the job, I applied for and was given the opportunity to obtain a RAF 'C' class driving licence, after taking a short road test with an MT Section NCO. This allowed me to drive the OCU Land Rovers on the station streets only; driving on civilian streets outside the station with only a 'C' licence was strictly forbidden.

Although I could drive reasonably well, I didn't have a civilian driving licence, so this was a great opportunity to get some driving experience without having to pay for lessons at a driving school and I certainly took advantage of every opportunity that arose to get behind the wheel. At the same time, under Gerry Gibson's mentorship and working in concert with Pete Thompson, my expertise and confidence as a Vulcan electrician steadily increased, such that I was often sent out to trouble shoot 'snags' by myself. That certainly helped the overall section, because Vulcans invariably landed with a laundry list of electrical snags that mostly needed to be rectified before the aircraft could go back into the air. Much of the time it was just something minor, like a blown fuse for one of the rear crew-members' angle-poise lamps, or to replace one of the two anti-dazzle light bulbs under the pilot's coaming. Other times, it would be a little more labour intensive, such as the replacement of a heavy Frequency Changer, two of which were mounted high up in the nose wheel bay. The Frequency Changer was a single machine that housed a motor and generator on the same shaft. The AC motor, powered by the aircraft's normal voltage and frequency, 200 volts, 400 Hz, turned the shaft and the AC generator at the other end of the shaft produced the necessary 115 volts, 1600 Hz for the radio and radar equipment. We electricians generally sat in on the crew technical debriefings after they returned from a sortie, to get first hand information on the nature of the snags.

***

Practising one's trade was only part of the duties that were expected of those us of us on what is known as first line servicing. Aircraft handling was also a major part of the work. This meant being part of starter crews, seeing in crews, refuelling crews, and generally moving ground equipment around the flight line to where it was needed. The latter was something I relished, since it usually meant towing items such as ground power units or Palouste aircraft starter units around the aircraft pans.

Starter and seeing-in crews consisted of three or four men, plus the aircraft crew-chief. For a start-up, a man was stationed at the two heavy ground power cables that were plugged into their respective sockets towards the aft underside end of the Vulcan. One cable carried the main 200 volts AC power supply while the other was a 28 volts DC supply for cockpit instruments, lighting and basic systems control functions. In the air, this supply would be derived from the main AC power supply, but was kept separate on the ground because it wasn't usually necessary to have the 200 volts power applied for normal servicing purposes. Another man stood by the Palouste engine starter cart waiting for the signal to start it. The Palouste consisted, basically, of a small jet engine and its supporting systems enclosed within the cart. Its control was slaved to Vulcan's engine start system. This ground crewman's job was to connect it to the Vulcan, start it up when needed, shut it down when no longer needed, disconnect it and get it out of the way. Each main wheel chock was attended by the third and fourth ground crew members, although on a three-man crew, either the Palouste operator or the man who removed the power cables would take charge of one of the chocks.

The Crew Chief stood by the nose wheel, his headphones plugged into a socket in the wheel bay through which he communicated with the aircrew via the aircraft intercom. The plug for his headphones was at the end of a very long lead that allowed him to move around a large area of the concrete pan on which the Vulcan sat.

When given the word by the captain, the Crew Chief gave the starter signal to the Palouste operator, who then started its small jet engine. From the cockpit, the captain initiated the number 1 engine start system which then proceeded through an automatic sequence of which an early step was to accelerate the Palouste. Compressed bleed air from the Palouste's compressor section surged into the engine's turbo-starter, via a flexible duct connected into an underwing inlet, accelerating the Olympus engine up to start speed. Meanwhile, the start system initiated the fuel igniter units that lit off the engine fuel in the combustion chambers, after the captain had opened up the engine fuel cock. The Palouste continued to assist the engine's acceleration until it achieved self-sustaining speed. At that stage in the sequence, the Palouste decelerated and the Crew Chief signalled for it to be shut down, disconnected and wheeled away to the side of the pan, clear of the aircraft. With number 1 engine running, the captain was now able to start the other engines by directing bleed air from the number 1 engine compressor through a cross flow valve and a network of selectable ducts and valves.

When all engines were up and running, the ground crew, now wearing ear defenders for protection from the deafening noise of the four mighty Olympus engines running just above their heads, waited for the next hand signals from the Crew Chief. On board, check-lists were being followed, one of which was for the AEO to bring the aircraft AC alternators on line. Once this had been done, he told the Crew Chief to disconnect the 200 volts ground power. A hand signal to the airman standing by the ground power cables directed him to pull the 200 volt umbilical cable out, an action that automatically tripped off the power at the ground power unit. The airman then closed the small hinged panel that protected the recessed power inlet plug and latched it closed with a quarter twist of its Dzuz fastener, making the panel flush with the fuselage. The Vulcan's main electrical power was now being provided by the engine-driven alternators, but the AEO needed to verify that all were providing the correct voltage and frequency before he connected them onto their bus-bars, so the ground power unit was still supplying 28 volts DC power at this stage. Having got the alternators on line, the AEO now started the transformer rectifier units, or TRUs, which provided a stepped-down, rectified 28 volts DC derived from the 200 volts AC bus-bars. Having done this, he informed the Crew Chief, who then signalled for the external 28 volt umbilical cable to be removed. The Vulcan was now fully independent of all ground equipment and ready to roll.

Taking instructions from the captain, through his head set, the Crew Chief gave the 'chocks away' signal – an energetic, repetitive, crossing and uncrossing of his two downward extended arms. Pulling on ropes attached to the chocks, the ground crewmen dragged the heavy chocks clear of the wheels. This left only the smaller nose wheel chock in position.

The Crew Chief then raised and stowed the crew access ladder from the still open aircrew compartment entrance door. After stowing the ladder, he pressed and held a button adjacent to the door, causing the two powerful pneumatic jacks attached to the door to operate, pulling the door upwards to close and seal the entrance hatch. Turning around, he indicated for the nose wheel chock to be removed, to which one of the ground crew immediately reacted by running forward to drag the chock to the side of the pan. After informing the captain that all was now clear of the aircraft, the Crew Chief unplugged his long lead, coiling it over his forearm as he moved laterally outwards from the Vulcan to where he would become visible to the captain and then gave him a 'thumbs up' gesture. The engines of the big jet now spooled up, brakes were released and it moved forward towards the taxiway, as those ground crew members still on the pan ducked behind items of ground equipment to shelter from the inevitable jet blast as the Vulcan exited the pan, on its way out to the runway. Well before this, one ground crew member would have picked up a pair of marshalling bats (or lighted wands if it was a night-time start), and positioned himself at the edge of the taxiway, opposite the pan.

When the marshaller saw the Crew Chief give the thumbs up, he raised up his bats, with both arms extended straight above his head, the flats of the bats facing towards the pilot. Then, when the Vulcan began to move, he commenced giving the 'come straight ahead' motion with his bats; both arms brought down to knee-height and then raised again until the bats almost came together behind his head, then down again, with the motion repeated continuously, all the while watching the nose wheel to keep it on the taxiway centreline. When it came time for the Vulcan to turn to its right onto the taxiway, the marshaller lowered the bat on the side to which the aircraft needed to turn while continuing to marshal with the other bat. When the turn was completed, he pointed with both bats towards the runway, which was only a short distance from the OCU dispersal at Finningley. Then, a final salute by raising one bat, the marshaller indicated that the pilot was now on his own.

The foregoing is a description of a 'normal' start of a B2 Vulcan, using a Palouste; however the Vulcan could also be started using the Airborne Auxiliary Power Plant, or AAPP. This was a small gas turbine installed within the wing of the aircraft. It served a dual purpose, the main one being to supply emergency electrical power in the case of loss of the main alternators due to a four-engine flame out – something that did happen on at least one rare occasion. Its other function was to perform engine starting at airfields where a Palouste was not available or for rapid engine starting on QRA aircraft. It was configured to start number 1 engine only and then, as with the Palouste, the three other engines were started using bleed air from number 1.

The AAPP was manufactured by the Rover Company, which was better known for its Rover cars. Because of this, it was more often referred to as 'the Rover' – easier to trip off the tongue than the awkward sounding AAPP (although the AAPP was sometimes referred to by nerdy types as the 'Ay squared, Pee squared').

***

The OCU was run on the same lines as a normal RAF squadron and as such, it was responsible for the 1st and 2nd line servicing on its aircraft. To facilitate this, the Unit was resident in an allotted hangar that not only contained the OCU offices, crew rooms, stores and operations room, but wherein the 2nd line servicing was performed. So, in addition to our line duties, starter crews, etc., OCU tradesmen were also involved in the more in-depth 2nd line servicing in the hangar, where we not only practised our own trade but participated in activities that involved pure manpower. Hangar floor sweeping being the least intellectually intensive of these, but also the least desired.

Undercarriage retraction tests were one of the operations performed in the hangar and for this, a Vulcan needed to be raised a few feet of the ground by means of hydraulic jacks. This is where all hands were called to the pumps, literally, because the jacks were manually operated by pumping up and down on long handles. The jacks themselves were, understandably, hefty items of equipment that stood on four legs that came out at an angle of around 20° from the body and terminated in frying-pan sized feet. Four jacks were required to raise a Vulcan, each placed at specific jacking points.

Many times, I was detailed to be on a crew to jack up a Vulcan, which was a highly choreographed process, one part of which never ceased to amuse me. It was necessary to raise the aircraft in small increments so that all jacks were sharing the load equally. If one jack had been raised even slightly higher than the others, it would have placed a heavier load on that jack, but also introduced unwanted stresses and strains on the airframe. It was the method by which this even load-sharing was achieved that I found amusing. The hydraulic rams of the jacks were threaded on their exterior, on which a similarly threaded collar had been installed. To begin with, each jack was raised until it just fitted into the aircraft jacking point. When all jacks were thus in place, their collars were screwed down until they made contact with the bodies of their jacks. The SNCO in charge of the operation then called out, "Up one." We then all began pumping the jacking handles, raising the collar off the body as the ram moved upwards. One of the men at each jack, usually an Airframes tradesman, held a pre-decimalization penny – the one bearing Britannia on one side and the sovereign in whose reign it was minted on the other. The penny measured about 1.22 inches (31 mm) in diameter. As the jack ram rose up, this man would hold the penny vertically against the growing gap between the collar and the jack body until the penny's diameter fitted into the gap. At that point he would tell the crew to stop pumping. When all four crews had ceased pumping and the in-charge SNCO was satisfied that he had got his penny-worth at each jack, he would then order that the collars on the jacks be screwed down to make contact with the jack body again. Then another "up one", by which he meant we were to jack up another penny diameter. By this means, the Vulcan was slowly and incrementally jacked up until the undercarriage was well clear of the hangar floor. Occasionally the SNCO, who was keeping an eye on the overall levelling datum and could therefore see if and when one end of the Vulcan was higher than the other, would call for just the front or rear jacks to be raised "up one" in order to make the necessary adjustment.

The same procedure was used in reverse when lowering the Vulcan, except that the order now was "down one," with the collars being screwed back up to a penny-width again each time they came down to make contact with the jack bodies. It always struck me as a little ludicrous that here we had an aircraft that was at the forefront of technology for its time, yet this crude, but effective method of raising and lowering the aircraft was employed instead of some high-tech method of keeping all four jacks rising and lowering in the same precise increments. I don't know how it was done after decimalization, because I wasn't involved in the process by that time, but I suspect that the old pennies were squirreled away in some secret hidey-hole.

Chapter 6: The Big Letdown

One day in November, a few of us on the Skybolt team were directed to report to the Orderly Room in Station Headquarters. There, we were issued with railway warrants and given the address of a tailor in London where we were to go to be measured for the special uniform we would wear while detached to the USAF Eglin AFB for the trials.

As the train approached London, it entered thick fog and on arrival at Kings Cross, the fog had developed into acrid smog. At that time, homes in the London area burned coal in their fireplaces and the smoke from this, together with diesel and petrol exhaust fumes from countless vehicles combined to form thick smog that burned my throat as I breathed it in. At the tailor's shop, there were a few other members of the Skybolt team, some of whom I knew, who had travelled from different stations to be there. It seemed that because Eglin Air Force Base in Florida, where the trials were to be held, was a sub-tropical location, we would be wearing tropical dress for much of our time there. The RAF was not too keen on the idea of us wearing the ugly standard issue Khaki Drill (KD) uniforms, which would have contrasted negatively with our counterparts in the USAF, so had decided that we would have specially made uniforms that would be a better reflection of our service and country.

The tailors took all the necessary measurements and told us, before we left, that we would be called back again in a few weeks for a fitting. Normally, I enjoyed being in the big city of London, but my throat felt raw and hurt so badly from the smog that I headed back to Kings Cross as soon as possible and caught the next train to Doncaster.

***

Winter set in with a vengeance. The snow that fell and was heaped along the sides of streets and roads turned to solid ice that remained there for several weeks. It wasn't all bad, because driving the Land Rover on the slippery snow and ice on large empty expanses of the taxiways helped teach me how to control a vehicle in those kinds of conditions. But my time at Finningley was coming to an end. The plan was to leave for Eglin early in the New Year. For this reason, I went on embarkation leave back to my family home in Coleraine, Northern Ireland. The embarkation leave also happened to coincide with the Christmas holiday period, when I would probably have gone home anyway.

On arriving home on leave, I was full of talk of my upcoming posting to Florida and on my bringing the subject up, my stepmother produced a letter that I had written to her some weeks previously. She showed me that the envelope had been stamped with a notation that it had been opened and censored. On the letter itself, some words and sentences had been blacked out. So now I knew which letter the Security Services people had intercepted, although I was taken aback that they would go to such lengths as part of the positive vetting process.

Relaxing and enjoying what would be my last visit home for probably a couple of years, I was blissfully unaware of the high level political shenanigans that were taking place right then about the future of Skybolt. Then, just before Christmas, it was announced on a television news broadcast that Prime Minister Harold Macmillan and President Kennedy had jointly agreed to cancel the Skybolt project in favour of equipping the Royal Navy with submarine-launched Polaris missiles. Family members asked how this was going to affect me and the simple answer was that I didn't know, but right then, I was in denial. This couldn't be happening! For the first time in my life, I was anxious for my leave to end so that I could get back to Finningley and find out what was going on.

Supposedly, according to psychologists, there are five stages of grief that individuals go through when something tragic occurs in their lives, such as the death of a loved one or the revelation that the individual is suffering from a terminal illness: Denial, Anger, Bargaining, Depression and, finally, Acceptance. The news that a plum posting to Florida has been cancelled isn't anywhere near as tragic as the aforementioned life events, but I believe that I actually went through a similar grieving process, although not all five – I skipped the bargaining and depression stages.

On returning to Finningley, the 'Denial' stage was soon put to bed when it was confirmed that we would definitely not be going to Eglin. An advance party had already been there for a few weeks and had sent newspaper ads showing the cheapness and availability of second hand cars, amongst other good things about the area. Those and the prospect of spending an extended length of time escaping the miserable winters and dodgy summers of the British climate in the warmth of Florida brought on the next grieving stage, anger; anger at Macmillan and Kennedy – the latter for killing the Skybolt and the former for agreeing to the cancellation. Perhaps, however, the RAF would let me stay at Finningley, where I was reasonably happy working with people that I got along with. It seemed to be working out that way, but unseen wheels were grinding and it wasn't to be. At least, I was able to stay there until early March 1963, but then I was given a posting to 50 Squadron, RAF Waddington.

Every cloud has its silver lining, so although I would have preferred to have remained at Finningley, the posting to Waddington was not unwelcome. To begin with, it was a posting to a 'real' squadron; something that had eluded me up to now in my RAF career. At Cranwell, it was the Royal Air Force College, not a squadron, and at Finningley it was an Operational Conversion Unit. I had long wanted to belong to a squadron that had an identity, a history, a squadron crest and the expected, legendary 'squadron spirit' that I had often heard about. It seemed that the time for this had finally arrived.

But there was another more important reason that Waddington was a welcome posting. There was a Lincoln girl who I was very keen on. We had met and started going out in March 1959, but then after two years, she came to the conclusion that I was being too serious and she didn't want to be tied down just yet, but instead she said she needed a bit more freedom, so she broke off the romance in April 1961. We had, however, stayed in touch with each other by the occasional letter or chatted when we accidentally bumped into each other (which was not always an accident on my part). After breaking up, I had dated other girls, but my Lincoln girl, her name was Pam, was always the standard by which I judged all others; none of them ever quite measured up. So I felt that my posting to Waddington would take me back to the Lincoln area and possibly the chance of starting afresh with Pam. I didn't let her know, though, that I would be returning. That was to be a surprise.

Chapter 7: Waddington

I arrived at Waddington on March 5, 1963 and went through the standard 'blue chit' arrival process that everyone has to suffer when posted to a new station. For the uninitiated, it requires the new arrival to first visit the station orderly room to confirm that he or she has, in fact, turned up as ordered. After going through the preliminaries, the orderly room clerk presents the new arrival with a blue-coloured card on which to collect signatures from the various sections that need to know of the person's presence on the station, such as the bedding store, Catering section, and so on and so forth. Typically, there was a need to collect around twenty signatures in all, some of which had to be done in a certain order. One of the stops was at the section or squadron to which the new arrival was assigned. In my case, this was 50 Squadron, but I decided to leave this to the second day so that I could remain in a kind of twilight zone of having arrived but not quite arrived. I had other plans for the afternoon of the first day.

After lunch at the airmen's mess, I hurried back to the transit billet where I was temporarily housed and changed into my civvies, then caught a bus into Lincoln. My ultimate destination was Boot's the Chemist, where Pam worked as a shop assistant. Her face lit up when she saw me approaching her counter.

"What are you doing here?" She asked with a welcoming smile.

I broke the news that I had been posted to Waddington, so was back in town and then I asked her to meet me that evening. She consented, but also let me know that she was involved with someone else, so it would just be a friendly get-together. The fact that she even agreed to come out with me was good enough for me – for the moment. We met later for a drink at one of the many pubs in Lincoln and caught up with each other's news. Mine was about the posting to Florida being cancelled, which was why I was now at Waddington. Hers was about her current boyfriend, who, it turned out, was also in the RAF and stationed at Waddington. She told me his name and I made a mental note to avoid him if I found out where he worked. My spirits soared at being with her and that evening, while returning to the transit billet, it felt like I was walking on air.

The next morning, my second day of 'arriving', I showed up at my new squadron's orderly room, blue chit in hand, expecting to be warmly greeted as its newest member. However, instead of welcoming me to the bosom of the squadron, the Flight Sergeant to whom I presented myself informed me that I would not be joining 50 Squadron. Over my protests that that's where I had been posted, he explained, none too pleasantly, that the Station had recently adopted the concept of centralized servicing and that the three squadrons at Waddington, numbers 44, 50 and 101, no longer had their own servicing personnel. For the sake of efficiency, all servicing personnel had been combined into one large group under the Station Engineering Officer. First line servicing, the type performed on the aircraft engaged in day-to-day operations, was now the responsibility of the newly formed Flight Line Squadron, centred on E (or Echo) dispersal and this was where all first-line servicing personnel were posted.

Why was it named Flight Line Squadron, or 'Line Squadron' or, even more informally, just 'The Line' in normal parlance? The flight line on most RAF stations was literally a line-up of the operational aircraft on the aircraft pan – a concrete apron on the airfield. This was more typical of fighter or flying training stations, but the term 'The Line' has come to mean the site of operational aircraft on any station. So, although the Waddington aircraft were dispersed around the airfield on their individual dispersal pans, the 'Line' term still applied.

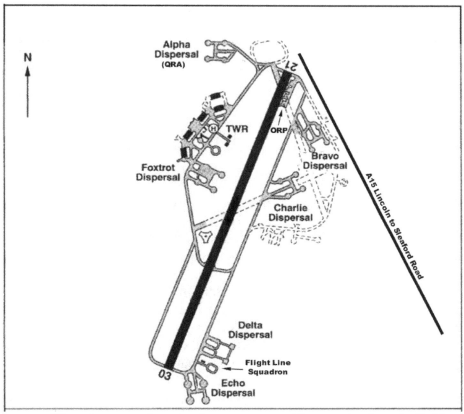

The aircrews, it turned out, were still organized as individual squadrons, but instead of having their aircraft at the previously squadron-dedicated dispersals, they were now allocated aircraft on any of the active dispersals, Charlie, Delta and Echo. Alpha dispersal was permanently dedicated to the three QRA aircraft and Bravo dispersal, the one nearest the A15 Lincoln to Sleaford road, where I had often seen Vulcans on my way to and from Cranwell, was now left fallow for some unknown reason.

Waddington also had a couple of other unpleasant surprises in store. All of its Vulcans were Mk B1A. For me, this was significant because I had been trained on the newer Mk B2 which had a completely different electrical system. Instead of a 200 volt AC system, the Mk B1A was powered by 112 volt DC generators that were not only controlled and organized in a completely different way to the 200 volt AC system, but the system's installation seemed a lot more haphazard, especially in the Power Compartment, when compared with the neatly arranged fuses and circuit breakers that characterised the B2 Power Compartment. Essentially, I had to learn a completely different system in order to be an effective technician.

With two strikes against my new posting, I then discovered the third; that Pam's boyfriend – my rival for her affections – was an Air Wireless corporal on Flight Line Squadron too and, not only that, but we were on the same Shift. This was going to be awkward!

Flight Line Squadron had its own fleet of Mechanical Transport, mostly Land Rovers, but also a few 1-ton lorries (One-Tonners) and RTVs, (Bedford vans designed to transport delicate radio and radar equipment) because it was almost the only way to get to and from E dispersal, which was off in a remote part of the airfield. At shift change times, there was a bus that left the airmen's mess and then returned with the retiring shift members, but at all other times it was a matter of either driving one of the vehicles yourself, or walking to the nearest part of the perimeter taxiway on the domestic side of the camp and thumbing a lift if you wanted to get out to Echo. Private transport could drive to and from the dispersal, but it was mostly by married personnel who lived off the camp and they could only use the privilege to get to and from work. The private cars had to remain parked at the dispersal at all other times.

Still carrying my blue chit, I walked out to the perimeter taxiway, thumbed a lift and arrived at the Flight Line Squadron where I was directed to the desk of the Admin NCO, Sergeant Renshaw, a smallish man with a dark, full moustache, who was not exactly beloved by the rank and file members of the squadron. Sergeant Renshaw added my name to the squadron strength and allocated a bed in Vulcan block, the 2-storey barrack block where the Line Squadron 'other ranks' were accommodated. 'A' shift had the bottom floor and 'B' shift was on the upper storey. The block was a fairly modern barrack, divided into rooms, each containing five beds. The room to which I was assigned was at the back of the building, overlooking the police dog kennels.

Back at Line Squadron, I was introduced to my workmates. Chief Technician Pete Diamond was the SNCO in charge of the electricians, assisted by corporals 'Ginge' Kingdom, 'Mitch' Mitchell, Jimmy Greenock and 'Chas' Chaplin. Fellow J/Ts were Stan Eilbeck, Geoff Supple, 'Butch' Butcher (who I already knew from our St. Athan Boy Entrant training) and SAC Barry Goodall. At first, my main occupation was to accompany the others on their servicing duties until I got a grasp of the unfamiliar B1A electrical system.

Although my initial reaction to being on Line Squadron was one of disappointment because it wasn't a 'real' squadron, as time went on, it turned out to be the best posting in all of my RAF service. Those with whom I made friends became friends for life. The work was hard and demanding, but we had a sense of all being in it together and so the camaraderie was great – the longed-for 'squadron spirit' existed, even if Flight Line Squadron wasn't of the traditional mould.

Chapter 8: Baby It's Cold Outside

On Flight Line Squadron, we worked a three-shift system. There was a normal Day and Night shift. Day shift began at 08:00 hours (8 am) and ended at 17:00 hours (5 pm). Night shift started at the same time that Day shift ended and lasted until 02:00 hours (2 am next morning). The shifts were known as 'A' and 'B' shifts and personnel were assigned on a permanent basis to each shift. The shifts worked one week of days and one week of nights, alternating between each shift, the first day of the working week being Monday. In addition to the normal day and night shifts, there was also a 'Swing' shift. This was basically a skeleton crew that came on shift at midnight and worked through to 08:00 when the day shift came on duty. Unlike 'A' and 'B' shifts, personnel were not permanently assigned to the Swing shift, but were detailed from members of that week's night shift. The main job for Swing shift was to get those aircraft that were earmarked for the next day's sorties ready to fly. That meant performing pre-flight inspections and fixing any outstanding snags. It wasn't the most popular shift because it meant sleeping through most of the next day. There was little time for a social life because, to get a full eight hours of sleep, which young men need, it was around 5 pm or 6 pm by the time we got up, performed our ablutions and got something to eat. With this kind of timetable, off-camp activities were impractical, so all that was left to do was go to the NAAFI or the camp cinema. Fortunately, the shift only lasted for one week and then those of us on it went back to normal shift duties.

***

By the time I arrived at Waddington, the worst of winter had passed, but it had been a bitterly cold one during my time at Finningley. There, we frequently had to de-ice the Vulcans and help clear snow from the dispersal areas, but the Finningley ground crew seemed to get off lightly compared to what the lads at Waddington were obliged to put up with. This was mainly because Waddington was a Master Diversion Airfield, but more about that later. Geoff Supple wrote an article describing the Waddington winter experience, which was originally published on the 'Vulcan to the Sky' website, <http://www.vulcantothesky.org/>, and reproduced below.

The really cold, Cold War

According to Wikipedia, January 1963 was the coldest month of the 20th century. As a young airman serving at RAF Waddington during that period I am not going to argue with them! It snowed heavily over the Christmas, and then the Big Freeze set in.

On returning from an extended Christmas Grant it was obvious that extreme measures would need to be taken to maintain the Master Diversion Airfield status. It was only 2 months since the Cuban Missile Crisis and it was essential that the runway and perimeter track remained operational. The Jet Snow Blowers hadn't found Lincolnshire, so it was down to manpower! By day we de-iced the aircraft and carried out our normal Flight Line duties. At night and during the early hours we were summoned by the infamous Tannoy to report for snow clearing tasks.

De-icing the aircraft procedures wouldn't have impressed today's H&S Executive. Donned in heavy Michelin Man looking suits we clambered off the De-icer truck roof and proceeded to spray the sticky Water Glycol solution over the Ailerons, Elevators, and anything that moved. It wasn't without its problems, as the surfaces became very slippery and the cold biting wind blew the liquid back into your face. Ugh!!

Cold weather clothing was scarce. I only had a furry jacket, it kept me warm, but an anorak with a hood would have been more welcome. Apparently, you could put your name down for an anorak and would receive one in due course; "When you were on the Frozen list," one of my friends remarked.

In the absence of Jet Snow Blowers, the preferred method of clearance was to be transported up and down the runway on the back of a 3 Tonner shovelling the grit into a towed hopper. Not a pleasant experience!

Rumours were abounding that a Rum Ration would be issued, but someone else must have been having mine!! Another task was to clear the thick ice between No 3 and No. 4 Hangars. Again, manpower was the order of the day. We nibbled away at the thick ice with every implement that we could find. I have a vague memory of an aircraft towing arm being buckled when the Tugmaster tried to extricate a Vulcan from No. 3 Hangar.

Mr. Khrushchev would have been having a quiet chuckle over his Vodka if he could have witnessed the antics over those cold, cold, Cold War days! But, all's well that ends well. The Station Commander assembled us all in No. 5 Hangar, gave us the Ol' 'Good Show Chaps' speech, failed to break open the Rum, but mentioned in passing, that, like the Windmill Theatre, we never closed ! Even London Airport (as it was called then) was down for 20 minutes.

Roll on May, Exercise Sunspot, I thought - you can keep your anorak....

When the winter wind from the east whistles across the flat Lincolnshire landscape, locals say that it's coming from Siberia and that "there's nothing between here and there but a barbed wire fence". That might be a bit of an exaggeration, but it got really cold out on the Line during the winter months. As Geoff Supple has remarked in his '*The really cold, Cold War*' article above, suitable cold weather clothing was in short supply during the winter of 1962/63. By the time the following winter arrived, the Flight Line Squadron storemen had managed to get on the ball and were able to make sure an adequate supply of good cold weather clothing was on hand. We were issued with hooded anoraks, warm working gloves and sweaters to those who wanted them. Also, a favourite with most were the thick, white sea-boot stockings and sturdy leather, commando-soled, lace-up boots that we nicknamed Trog Boots.

We were only supposed to wear this gear out on the Line and not around the domestic site, although a blind eye was turned to us wearing them between the airmen's mess and our barrack block. But the Station Warrant Officer was wont to turn bright red and tear his hair out if he spotted anyone walking around other parts of the camp clad in our oil-stained anoraks and Trog Boots.

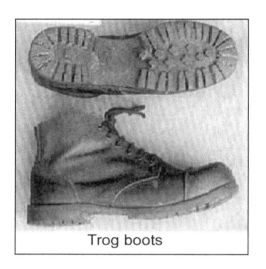

Trog boots

Chapter 9: A Romance Rekindled

Off camp, I was still interested in getting back with Pam, but in the meantime met up with another girl named Maureen and although she was pretty and had a sweet personality, I still compared her to Pam and Pam won the competition. By this time, I had identified Pam's boyfriend. He was a nice guy, so I didn't have any resentment towards him; just envy. Occasionally, I would bump into Pam in Lincoln and on one such meeting, she invited me to her 21st birthday party at her home where she lived with her parents, brother and sister. Her boyfriend was, of course, also invited, so it promised to be an interesting evening.

Although he recognized me from the squadron, he was unaware of my history with Pam, but during the party, we talked about it. Afterwards, neither of us had any transport to get back to camp and the Lincoln city buses had stopped running, as had the County buses, so we set off walking together to make our way back on foot, or until we could get to a location where it would be more likely to get a lift. During our walk, I told him how deeply I felt about Pam. He, in turn, said that he wasn't quite so committed and agreed to step aside and leave the way clear for me to resume my courtship of Pam…if she agreed, and I believed that she would. In the following days, she and I did resume our relationship and now that both of us were more mature, things were a lot better. Back at work, though, I suffered considerable acrimony from the now ex-boyfriend's work pals, who accused me of stealing his girlfriend. I countered by telling them that she had been my girlfriend first and that she and I were only taking up where we had left off. Eventually, the bad feelings subsided and the situation was accepted as the status quo.

Now, with frequent visits to Lincoln to see Pam, I really needed transport of my own, but with my meagre savings, I couldn't afford a car. The solution came by way of Corporal Chas Chaplin. He was married and lived off the camp and his mode of transport, when I first came to Line Squadron, was a Lambretta scooter-sidecar combination. He let it be known that the combination was up for sale, which quickly got my attention. I offered to buy the scooter, but said that I didn't want the sidecar. At first, he was reluctant to split up the combination, but then he found someone interested in the sidecar alone, so agreed to sell me the scooter, which served me well for quite some time afterwards. As well as providing me with the mobility to visit Pam in Lincoln, it was also instrumental in forging a friendship with Johnny Thorne, an Air Radio Fitter, who was also on 'A' Shift. Johnny's girlfriend, Carol, lived in the St. Giles area of Lincoln, as did Pam, and he also owned a scooter, although his was a Vespa and it was faster than my Lambretta. We found ourselves travelling back to Waddington around the same time on the evenings when we were on day shift and, from this, a lifelong friendship was born.

Chapter 10: An Electrician's Lot

Working on the Vulcan of either Mk as an electrician was satisfying, but challenging. Most aircraft returned from sorties with at least one electrical snag that frequently involved removing a faulty component and replacing it with a serviceable unit. This could be a heavy piece of equipment, such as a Rotary Transformer on the B1A that was basically a 112 volt DC motor and a 28 volt DC generator on the same shaft or, in the case of the B2, a Frequency Changer that performed a similar function, except that the motor was driven by 200 volts AC and the generator provided a 115 volts single phase 1600 Hz for the radio and radar equipment. In both cases, these units were securely bolted down onto an equipment shelf in the nose wheel bay; the B1A was equipped with three Rotary Transformers whereas the B2 had just two Frequency Changers. The B1A nose wheel bay also housed three large, heavy Type 350 Inverters that provided 115 volts AC for the radar equipment. Access to all of these machines was reasonably easy, but muscle power was needed to lift them into position or remove them and a contortionist's skill required to reach the rear bolts with spanner, which could only be turned one 'flat' at a time. A 'safety raiser' – an adjustable platform that could be raised and lowered by means of a manually operated hydraulic ram, was the best way to get up in there and work on them.

Geoff Supple recalls that when he first began working on Vulcans, he was helping another airman remove one of the Rotary Transformers. Metal ducting for the supply of cooling air to the machine first needed to be removed before anything else could be done. To overcome misalignment problems, the final coupling between the ducting and the Rotary Transformers was by means of a large rubber sleeve that was approximately 6" long, 4" in diameter and ¼" wall thickness. Both ends of the rubber sleeve were anchored to the throats of the ducting and the Rotary Transformer air inlet by means of hose clamps.

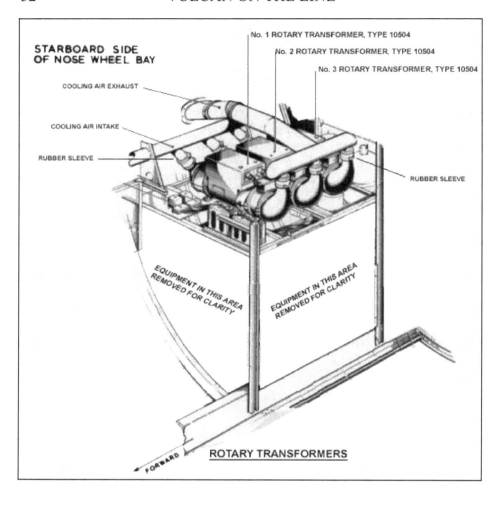

STARBOARD SIDE
OF NOSE WHEEL BAY

No. 1 ROTARY TRANSFORMER, TYPE 10504

No. 2 ROTARY TRANSFORMER, TYPE 10504

No. 3 ROTARY TRANSFORMER, TYPE 10504

COOLING AIR EXHAUST

COOLING AIR INTAKE

RUBBER SLEEVE

RUBBER SLEEVE

EQUIPMENT IN THIS AREA REMOVED FOR CLARITY

EQUIPMENT IN THIS AREA REMOVED FOR CLARITY

FORWARD

ROTARY TRANSFORMERS

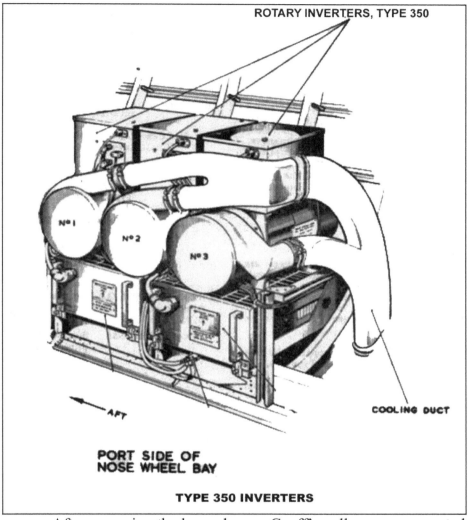

ROTARY INVERTERS, TYPE 350

N° 1
N° 2
N° 3

AFT

COOLING DUCT

PORT SIDE OF NOSE WHEEL BAY

TYPE 350 INVERTERS

After removing the hose clamps, Geoff's colleague commented on how difficult it was to remove the rubber sleeves because, after removing the clamps, the rubber tended to be very tightly bonded to the metal ducting. Anyone who has ever had to remove a car's radiator hose will immediately understand this problem. The airman proceeded to demonstrate his method for its removal by pushing a GS screwdriver blade between the sleeve and the ducting and then, using all his strength, forced the GS blade in an upward direction to try to free the sleeve. Unfortunately, the rubber suddenly gave up the fight by splitting at the point of leverage. The suddenly unrestrained GS blade sprang in an upward direction only stopping when it reached the airman's forehead. Quite a lot of blood and plenty of impolite language issued forth from the hapless bloke, who probably retained a perfect screwdriver indentation on his forehead for the remainder of his days. As for Geoff, the experience taught him to use copious amounts of Hellerine (a special lubricant normally used to facilitate the application of rubber insulating sleeves onto electrical cables) prior to attempting the removal of the ducting sleeves.

Other smaller inverters that supplied alternating current for a variety of electronic equipment were located in various places within the crew compartment and, while they didn't require superhuman strength to install or remove, were invariably located in difficult to reach locations that called for much contortion and exclamations of colourful language during those operations.

The alternators on a B2 and the generators on a B1A were driven from an auxiliary gearbox on the engine, so removal was by the Engine tradesmen, but we electricians needed to be in attendance to disconnect the cables or reconnect them when a replacement item was being installed.

As an aside, the AC alternator on the B2 was driven by an amazing device that kept the alternator turning at a constant speed and thus able to produce a constant 400 Hz frequency, regardless of the speed at which the engine was turning; frequency being directly related to the alternator's rotational speed. The device was known as the Sunstrand Constant Speed Drive (manufactured by the Sunstrand Company). It was purely mechanical, employing hydraulic fluid to rotate an internal component faster or slower, depending on the speed at which the engine was operating. The output drive of this internal device is what drove the alternator. Speed didn't matter with the B1A generator because it produced DC voltage which wasn't affected by engine speed.

Most other electrical 'black box' components, as well as the aircraft batteries were located in the Power Compartment, often crammed into almost inaccessible locations. This compartment was located at the aft end of the aircraft and was accessed by a hinged hatch that was held closed by two latches. The hatch was about seven feet above ground level on a B1A and probably eight feet on a B2 because of the difference in the height between the nose wheel legs of both types. When the latches were undone, the hatch swung downwards on its hinges, allowing an airman to climb up inside. The interior walls of the compartment were festooned with physically large high-amperage fuses, circuit breakers and other items. The black boxes, (voltage regulators, load controllers, jet pipe temperature controllers and such) were arrayed at lower levels. A flat deck plate provided enough room for no more than two people to work in the compartment, which was illuminated by dome type servicing light on the ceiling that came on automatically when 28 volts DC ground power was applied to the aircraft, but was turned off when the aircraft was providing its own power; a factoid that will have significance later in the narrative.

Probably the most difficult job involving the Power Compartment had to do with manhandling the heavy aircraft batteries in and out of there. Unlike car batteries, which typically remain installed in the car until they die, aircraft batteries were removed at regular intervals for servicing and replaced with others that had been serviced and fully charged. There was a total of five 24 volt nickel cadmium batteries, four of which were connected in series to act as a 96 volt battery supply to the 112 volt DC system. The fifth battery was a 24 volt battery that provided a supply for the aircraft 28 volt DC electrical system. The 96 volt batteries squatted at the aft end of compartment and the 24 volt battery was located nearby against the port bulkhead.

The batteries were heavy, 76 lbs. each, and bulky, so the job of removing them was, by itself, a challenging task in the confines of the Power Compartment where there was only enough room for one man to access them. First, he had to unclip and remove a lid that protected the 96 volt batteries and then cut through the locking wire that prevented the connectors from coming undone in flight due to vibration. Locking wire was vicious stuff! The ends, when snipped off by a previous installer, were razor sharp and could slice through unprotected skin with the ease of a surgeon's scalpel. Personally, when installing it, I always turned the ends of my locking wire back on itself so that those sharp ends wouldn't be sticking out to lacerate someone, including myself. Not everyone extended such a courtesy however, so it was common for an unwary person to make painful and bloody contact with those sharp ends. The 24 volt battery was housed under a separate cover, but it was of the same type of battery as those that comprised the

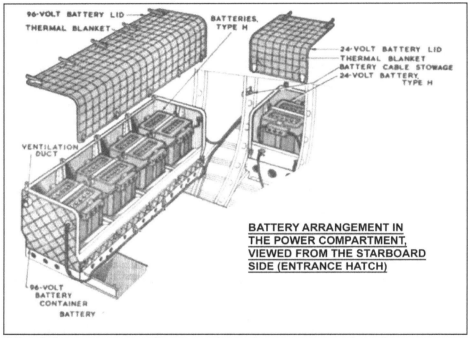

96 volt battery, so was just as awkward to remove as the others.

        Next the old batteries needed to be removed from the Power Compartment, which was a task that required at least two electricians in order to manhandle them out of the small hatch and down a step ladder. The process was then played out in reverse by lifting the new batteries into the compartment, installing and connecting them, including much twisting of locking wire before the job was complete. But, as electricians, we couldn't complain too much because other trades had much worse things to do. Engine fitters had to crawl up the jet pipe to inspect the rear turbine blades. On re-emerging, they were usually covered in soot and looked like chimney sweeps. The Airframes lads had the unpleasant task of emptying aircrew members' 'pee' bladders (there was no toilet on board a Vulcan), when such members didn't have the decency to empty their own. More about pee bladders later.

The bolts holding the black boxes in place, usually four in number that were located on the underside of the component, near its corners, in many cases were difficult to access and could only be felt rather than seen. In addition, the restricted access often meant that the range of movement of a socket wrench or spanner was very limited. Because of the difficulty, there was always the danger of dropping a bolt or a tool into an almost inaccessible nook or cranny. Leaving a loose article in an aircraft was a major no-no, so the item had to be retrieved, even if it meant calling in airframe tradesmen to assist. We often joked that God should have equipped us with double and triple jointed fingers to allow us to get at these difficult bolts. In moments of frustration, we loudly and frequently cursed the designers of the aircraft with such expressions as, "The bastard who designed this should be made to come and take it out!"

Something I learned early on when working on aircraft, the hard way I might add, was to suppress the knee-jerk reaction of trying to catch something as it fell, but rather to watch where it ended up. Trying to catch a small falling object, such as a nut or bolt, risked batting it away into some unknown nook or cranny. Watching where it fell, on the other hand, meant that its location was known and was therefore a huge advantage in retrieving it. This also works well in everyday life.

Having toured the Avro factory, I knew in my heart why the design engineers had placed the black boxes where they were. The Vulcan was fabricated in large modules, at different Avro factories and the designers were unaware that when two modules were bolted together at the Woodford factory, accessible equipment could be blocked off by the structure of an adjoining module.

It wasn't just small nuts and bolts that could cause a problem as a loose article; the following story was related to me by George 'Mitch' Mitchell, one of the electrical fitter corporals with whom I worked on Line Squadron at Waddington.

"One day," says Mitch, *"I went to the electrical cupboard to get something and noticed the generator ground-run multimeter (commonly called an AVO because of its ability to measure Amps, Volts and Ohms) was missing. I asked the Chief Tech in charge of our electrical group, a large man with a mop of grey hair, but he knew nothing of it. Thinking that it might have been left in an aircraft's Power Compartment, I sent the lads out to check all of the Vulcans on the 'D' and 'E' dispersals and then asked 'Clutch' Goodall to drive me down to 'C' dispersal in a Land Rover, so that we could check the aircraft down there. At one particular Vulcan, after I had climbed a step ladder and entered the Power Compartment to look for the AVO, the Crew Chief, a particularly unpleasant Master Technician, came to the bottom of the steps and demanded to know what I was doing in 'his' aircraft. I replied that I was looking for the missing AVO. He retorted angrily that if I found it in his aircraft, he would put me on a charge. I just looked at 'Clutch' and commented that that particular Crew Chief was a fruit and nut case and then went over to another aircraft. The missing AVO eventually turned up and did not become a pathetic loose article in some Vulcan."*

Chapter 11: Let Me Outta Here!

The Power Compartment on one particular Vulcan nearly became the scene of a fatality that was, thank God, miraculously averted. A corporal electrician and a young, diminutive electrical mechanic named Dick Lowther, were in the compartment one night, rectifying a 'crew-in snag'; an electrical problem that had manifested itself with the aircrew on board and with the engines running.

Crew-in snags were the worst kind of fault because of the pressure to get the problem solved and prevent the sortie from being aborted. The Crew Chief, in particular, was the one who applied most pressure in those kinds of situations. He wanted the Vulcan to be airborne and out of his hair. An aborted sortie meant more work for him, whereas a launched aircraft meant that he could relax for a few hours or maybe even go home.

The corporal had fixed the problem, or so he thought and by rights, he should have made sure that the entire job was complete before taking care of the paperwork. But because of the heightened sense of urgency, he climbed out of the Power Compartment and made his way towards the Crew Chief's 'igloo' at the edge of the pan to 'clear' the snag in the Form 700 (the aircraft's maintenance log), leaving young Dick to replace 'black box' covers and tidy-up in the Power Compartment. Meanwhile, the Crew Chief, busy doing other things while talking to the crew through his headset and 'long lead', turned around and saw the corporal walking towards the igloo. He also perceived that the Power Compartment hatch was still open and so moved towards it, all the while talking to the aircrew. Stepping up on the step ladder that the pair of electricians were using for access to the compartment, he testily slammed the hatch closed and latched it without looking inside; he then took the step ladder away. In his anxious mind, the work had been completed and the aircraft was ready to taxi.

The corporal, having completed the paperwork, stepped out of the igloo and noticed that the Power Compartment hatch was closed and the ladder removed, so he assumed that Dick Lowther had finished the job and was now on his way back to the crew room. Inside the Power Compartment, the young electrician banged on the hatch with the handle of a screwdriver and shouted for attention, but no one could hear him above the roar of the engines. The ground power was removed causing the servicing light to go out, plunging the interior of the compartment into darkness, so the only illumination he had was a torch. He knew that he was almost certainly facing death from lack of oxygen and the freezing cold temperature if the Vulcan climbed to its operational altitude, but all the banging and shouting did no good. No one could hear him.

Meanwhile on the flight deck, the captain was preparing to taxi the aircraft to the runway, but the AEO was still unhappy because it appeared that the electrical problem was still present and so he advised the captain to abort the sortie. Begrudgingly, the captain cut the engines and the ground crew moved to replace the wheel chocks and re-apply the ground power. It was only then that one of them heard banging and hammering coming from the direction of the Power Compartment. Hastily, he brought a step ladder over from the edge of the pan, climbed up and released the hatch, whereupon a pale, frightened Lowther almost tumbled down the ladder in his eagerness to escape from his erstwhile prison. A few moments later, the crew compartment door swung down and the crew began to descend the door-mounted ladder. As they did so, one of the ground crew, an Air Radio mechanic who was well known for being something of a loudmouth, laughingly commented to the captain that he had nearly had a passenger on board for the sortie. Not fully understanding the comment, the seasoned Squadron Leader, smiling thinly, asked the airman what he meant. Still thinking it was a huge joke, the Air Radio explained what had happened. The Squadron Leader, in stark contrast, didn't quite see the funny side of it. He at first turned pale and then an angry red as he demanded an explanation from the Crew Chief. The Crew Chief sputtered something about thinking there was no one in the Power Compartment when he closed the hatch, but the Squadron Leader wasn't having it. The upshot was that the Crew Chief was summoned to appear before the Station Commander where he was severely and officially reprimanded for his serious and almost fatal blunder.

Later in conversation with Dick Lowther, a few of us, his fellow electricians, asked him what he would have done had the captain not aborted the sortie. He said that he would have started removing fuses and tripping circuit breakers so that equipment on the aircraft would cease working, which would then have forced the crew to abort. But I personally wondered if he would have had the cool-headedness to take such action, or would panic have taken over. Remember, the dome light in the compartment turned off when the ground power supply was removed and the aircraft was providing its own electrical power, so the hapless young man was in complete darkness. He had a torch, but it must have been very scary for him to be plunged into sudden darkness and then realize what was happening.

Chapter 12: The Landing Lamp Lesson

A Vulcan returned one night with an unserviceable port landing lamp. I drew the short straw and was sent out to Echo dispersal to sort out the problem. Probably a blown fuse, I thought – an easy fix and then back to the warmth and relative comfort of the crew room, our refuge from the chilly night air.

Sitting in the co-pilot's seat, I flicked the landing lamp switch to 'Land' and then to 'Taxi' while watching out through the windscreen to see what happened. The starboard landing lamp's beam tracked forward, first as a brilliant spotlight moving across the concrete of the dispersal as the lamp extended and finally pointed off into the now floodlit area in front of the Vulcan. But that was only on the starboard side of the aircraft; there was no matching beam of light from the port side. Flicking the switch to 'off', I clambered down the narrow ladder that led from the flight deck into the rear-crew members' compartment, where fuse panels 3P and 4P were located, only to find that the landing lamp circuit fuse wasn't a blown. It was beginning to look as though it wouldn't be such an easy fix after all.

Climbing back up the ladder and in the co-pilot's seat, I again switched the landing lamps back to the 'Taxi' position and left it there before descending the flight deck ladder and then down the entrance/exit ladder. The object now was to go outside and see if the port lamp had extended from its housing in the wing. From the bottom of the crew entrance door and in the glow of the sodium lights that surrounded the dispersal, I could see a dark shape poking down from underneath the Vulcan's port wing. The landing lamp had extended as it was supposed to, but the lamp wasn't on. Probably a failed bulb, I thought, but it could also have been an unserviceable micro switch within the assembly. In any event, it wasn't something that could be fixed in situ. The whole landing lamp assembly needed to be removed and sent to the Electrical Servicing Bay in the Electronics Centre for proper fault diagnosis and rectification. My task now was to remove it and replace it with a serviceable Landing Lamp assembly. Not a big problem – I had performed this job on a Vulcan before, while stationed at RAF Finningley.

The landing lamp was an integral part of a square panel which, when fitted into place, became part of the Vulcan wing's lower surface. The whole assembly – panel with the landing lamp still in place – needed to be removed and replaced with an identical assembly. At Finningley, the panel had been fastened in place by means of a gazillion Dzus fasteners – just a quarter turn anticlockwise with a GS screwdriver and the fastener was undone, or so I thought, but that was my second mistaken assumption of the night.

Going over to the Crew Chief's 'igloo', I notified him of my intention. He then got on the 'squawk box' to the squadron office to order a serviceable landing lamp from stores. Next, with GS screwdriver in hand, I ascended a step-ladder to tackle the Dzus fasteners, only to find that they weren't Dzus fasteners at all; the panel was held in place by a series of countersunk screws. This was a B1A Vulcan – those at Finningley were B2s. Evidently, when it came to designing the later and greater Vulcan Mk. B2, the Avro design engineers must have listened to some of the moans and groans of earlier servicing personnel about such things as replacing screws with the more maintenance-friendly Dzus fasteners. This was one example of the need for such a design change, which had apparently been implemented on the B2. However, the cold reality of this situation was that I was facing an equally large number of unfriendly screws instead. In fact, the panel was approximately 2 feet square and held in place by quarter inch diameter, half inch long, finely threaded, countersunk screws that were spaced at approximately 1 inch centres (2.5 cm.) around the perimeter of the panel, numbering approximately 88 screws. Their removal and then replacement represented a Herculean task, especially since the panel was above my head on the wing's underside, making the job even more onerous because it would mean craning to look upwards, with arms upheld and always the prospect of dropping a screw and losing it in the darkness, sodium lights around the pan not withstanding.

At this point, I should have called for a Rigger, but good luck with that! Waiting around for someone to remove and replace the panel would have taken much longer and besides, I didn't need to endure the verbal abuse that would no doubt have been hurled my way by whoever was assigned to the job. No, I would just get on with it – the sooner it was done, the sooner I could get back into the warmth of the crew room. All it needed was a pump action screwdriver and some elbow grease.

After maybe half an hour of being perched on the stepladder, a crick in my neck from craning upwards and arms aching from pumping the screwdriver at an upwards angle, the screws were all removed and the landing lamp assembly safely in my hands. By this time, the replacement assembly had been delivered to the dispersal, so I raised it up into place and made the electrical connection. However, having done battle with all of those screws, I decided not to put all of them back just yet, but use just enough of them to keep the assembly temporarily in place. I wanted to make sure that the new lamp worked before going through all that again. And so, a screw was inserted into the hole at each of the four corners of the panel, which was enough to hold it in place until I could carry out a functional test.

Returning to the co-pilot's seat on the flight deck, I flicked the switch to 'Land' and was now rewarded by twin beams of light that arced across the ground, then rose up to shine like two giant car headlights on main beam stabbing into the surrounding darkness. Flushed with the satisfaction of having rectified the snag, I clambered down out of the Vulcan and hurried across to let the Crew Chief know. He too was pleased and got me to clear the entry in the Form 700. But I needed an over-signature before it could be cleared entirely, so headed back into the squadron office to inform the Senior Technician 'Geordie' King, the SNCO Electrical Fitter who had sent me out to take care of the snag in the first place.

Geordie was new to the squadron and I wanted to make a good impression on him by proving my competence as a tradesman. On reaching the dispersal, I started walking towards the aircraft crew entrance, thinking that he would want to carry out a functional check, but no – he wanted to look at the landing lamp itself. I felt a bit annoyed by this, but realized he didn't know me well enough to trust me to do the job. I muttered something about there being no need and that everything was fine, but he ignored me and kept on walking towards the landing lamp location, so I just followed him. When we arrived at a point underneath the landing lamp both of us looked up. My feeling of annoyance very quickly changed to one of acute embarrassment. The landing lamp was in place all right, but the panel was only held in place by the four 'temporary' screws and staring down at us, like so many empty eye sockets, were the 80 or more holes that should have contained the remainder of the panel screws. An unprintable exclamation was my immediate reaction, at which point Geordie treated me to a scornful look while suggesting, in somewhat colourful language, that I finish the job before dragging him out into the cold night air again. With that, he turned on his heel and headed back towards the office.

I learned an important lesson that night. The slogan, *"Don't Assume – Check!"* that I had heard so often during trade training – and seen so often on flight safety posters and in the *'Air Clues'* magazine – took on a very personal meaning for me as a result of the incident. Never again did I question an NCO's responsibility to inspect my work before over-signing for it. Later, as an NCO myself, I made a point of never assuming but always checking when it came to over-signing someone else's work. Occasionally I would come across a cocky young airman, not unlike an earlier version of myself, who 'knew it all' and resented my oversight. Almost as often I would be able to give him a practical demonstration, based on his very own work, as to why such oversight was a necessary feature of our work as aircraft technicians.

Before moving on, just a final word on the topic of *"Don't Assume – Check!"* posters; there was a memorable 'cheeky' one, (reproduced overleaf from the last page of this chapter), which was very popular with the lads, for obvious reasons. The story goes that after it had been distributed to a number of stations, the Chief of Air Staff caught sight of it one day while on a visit to one particular station. He was prudishly displeased with it and ordered that it be taken down forthwith and that all copies be recalled and destroyed. Shortly thereafter, his unhappiness with the poster was strongly impressed on the then Director of Flight Safety whose previously unimpeded RAF career advancement suddenly and mysteriously came to a screeching halt.

Another well-liked poster featured Fred the Wheel Tapper. For those not in the know, a wheel-tapper was a railway employee who, armed with a long handled hammer, walked alongside a stationary train, tapping each wheel with his hammer as he progressed. A sound wheel would ring like a bell, but a cracked wheel would give off a dull sound. The poster cited that Fred condemned 534 wheels before discovering that his hammer was cracked. That particular poster was directed more at reminding servicing personnel to ensure that their test equipment was functioning correctly and properly calibrated before determining that item of equipment or system under test was faulty.

BE SAFE ~ don't assume

...CHECK!

Chapter 13: Role Change

V-bombers carried no defensive armament; the original B1 relied instead on its ability to fly at an altitude of 55,000 feet, far above the reach of enemy fighters and missiles of that time. Later, electronics countermeasures (ECM) were added to counteract the increased capabilities of Soviet air defences and this became the B1A, with the bulbous extension to the tail end that contained the ECM electronics being the most obvious superficial difference between it and the B1. The same philosophy and bulbous extension was continued with the introduction of the B2. Then, in 1960, an American U-2 reconnaissance aircraft, flying at an altitude of 65,000 feet, was downed by a Russian anti-aircraft missile. This news caused the Top Brass to rethink the role of the V-bombers and as a result, the high altitude profile was changed to one of low level penetration of the enemy territory, thereby avoiding radar detection. To make visual detection more difficult, the top side of the bombers was to be painted in a camouflage pattern although the white anti-flash finish was to be retained on the underside.

When I left Finningley in March 1963, the repainting had not been implemented on the 230 OCU Vulcans, or on the Waddington aircraft. But shortly after my arrival at Waddington, the station painters had applied a camouflage pattern to one of the aircraft. Unfortunately, possibly due to miscommunication or someone's Gung-ho attitude, they applied it in a random pattern, which was contrary to the Air Ministry's intent because the required pattern was anything but random; every Vulcan's pattern was to be identical to all of the others. The Vulcan was promptly dispatched to RAF St. Athan, where all of the repainting was supposed to be done on a planned timetable. Around the same time, the V-bomber force began practising low level flying, although the airframes were not entirely suited to the rough ride that resulted from flying in denser, more turbulent air.

Flying at low level may have helped the V-bombers to avoid enemy radar detection, but it introduced a brand-new hazard. In June 1963, one of our Waddington Vulcans, XH477, was lost while on a night time, low level practice sortie. It failed to clear a hill in the Scottish Highlands. Sadly, all five crew members lost their lives in the

accident. On that occasion, I remembered how anxious we all felt when its return was overdue. We talked amongst ourselves, expressing hope that it had merely been diverted to another airfield, possibly because of some urgent problem that required an immediate landing. But when no news came, those of us on night shift that evening became increasingly despondent in anticipation of the worst. Eventually, we heard about the accident and the fate of the crew. With the news, an air of gloom descended. The joking and repartee that typified our usual crew room atmosphere ceased, replaced by one of hushed conversation and sombre countenances.

One year and one month later, on a July day in 1964, information filtered down to those of us on The Line that another of our Vulcans, XA909, had crashed; this time in Wales. However, the news of the crash in Wales was better than on that of the previous Scottish loss. On this occasion, all crew members were able to abandon the doomed aircraft after it suffered a catastrophic number 4 engine failure that also took out the number 3 engine and partially disabled the aileron controls. In fact, this was the first time in Vulcan history that all of the rear crew members were able to escape. Prior to this disastrous event, it was only the pilots who managed to survive stricken Vulcans, thanks to their ejection seats. The rear crew members did not have ejection seats and in order to escape, had to get out of their seats wearing a bulky parachute pack, get the cabin entrance door open (which now doubled as an escape hatch) and slide down into the slipstream.

The crash in Wales was due to an overheated number 2 bearing in the number 4 engine. The bearing eventually failed, precipitating catastrophic damage to the engine. Compressor blades, flung off the damaged engine, penetrated the bulkhead between it and its neighbouring engine, causing that engine also to fail catastrophically. Blades from the failed number 3 engine then penetrated the bulkhead between its engine bay and the bomb bay, damaging the electrical wiring to the aileron powered flying controls to such an extent that the Vulcan was barely controllable.

The incidence of overheated number 2 bearings had become such a recurring problem that a modification came out which applied temperature detectors to the bearings, which were wired to a set of temperature gauges set into the AEO's table where he could keep an eye on them. This, however was a late attempt at managing the problem after a number of nasty incidents, one of which I witnessed first-hand when a Vulcan returned one day with its two port side engines flamed out. The aircraft's landing approach for this condition, known as an asymmetric approach, was practised regularly. It was commonplace to see a Vulcan coming in to land in an almost crabwise configuration because one pair of engines, either the two port or the two starboard, were throttled back to idling. This caused the aircraft to be skewed around its horizontal axis, presenting an angled attitude to the runway centreline. On this particular occasion, it was the real thing because both port engines had suffered the same catastrophic failure as the Vulcan that had crashed in Wales. In this case, however, the controls were spared and the aircraft was able to make a safe, asymmetric landing. This particular aircraft did not have a periscope installed, which, had there been one, would have allowed the AEO to view the upper and lower surfaces of the aircraft, so it is realistic to assume that the crew were unaware of the extent of the damage. Later that day, I visited the hangar into which the Vulcan had been pulled and saw that there was a large, oblong hole, clear through from the underside of the wing to the topside through which a man could easily have climbed. I was also told that when the captain deplaned and came around to look at the damage, he nearly fainted from shock. That particular crew was very lucky to get back on the ground in one piece.

After the installation of temperature gauges, the incidents came to an end. Presumably, if the AEO observed that the bearing temperature on any particular engine was rising beyond a safe value, the engine was promptly shut down.

Chapter 14: JFK Drops In To Waddington

One Saturday afternoon in June 1963, while most of we Waddington denizens were pursuing our weekend off-duty activities, a sleek Boeing 707, dressed in white, blue and silver livery, quietly touched down on the main runway. It carried a very special VIP who was making a brief private and unheralded stopover at the station.

The following report, (lightly edited), appeared in the Irish Post on July 3, 1963, (https://www.irishpost.com/news/jfk-derbyshire-detour-8224)

When President John F. Kennedy left Ireland for Britain on June 29th, 1963, he made a largely undocumented detour to Derbyshire to lay a wreath on the grave of his late sister Kathleen Kennedy.

At the time most observers believed the American President was travelling direct from Shannon to a meeting in London with British Prime Minister Harold Macmillan. But on June 29, 1963, Kennedy landed at the Royal Air Force base at Waddington, Lincolnshire and then travelled by helicopter to Edensor, Chatsworth in the Peak District.

His sister Kathleen had first come to London in 1938 before settling and marrying William Cavendish, the Marquis of Hartington. But after losing her husband in World War II she remarried a wealthy British aristocrat named Peter Fitzwilliam, who was the 8th Earl Fitzwilliam.

Tragedy struck again in May 1948 when on their way to a romantic getaway in the South of France via a meeting with her father Joseph Kennedy in Paris. En route, their small chartered plane crashed in stormy weather killing them both.

More than 15 years later on that June 1963 day in Derbyshire President Kennedy stood with another sister together with the Duke and Duchess of Devonshire and laid a wreath of flowers, which he brought from Ireland, on the grave.

Today, beneath an epitaph which reads: 'Joy she gave, Joy she has found' an acknowledgement states that Kathleen Kennedy was the 'Widow of the Major Marquis Hartington killed in action and daughter of the Hon. Joseph Kennedy sometime Ambassador of the United States to Great Britain'.

An added plaque reads: 'In memory of John F Kennedy, President of the United States of America who visited this grave on 29th June 1963'.

The following is an excerpt copied from The Star on-line newspaper, (https://www.thestar.co.uk/news/retro-peak-district-trip-by-president-kennedy-to-sister-s-grave-1-7163058).

At about 4.10 pm on Saturday June 29, 1963, the President of the United States, John F Kennedy, whirled into the village of Edensor in Derbyshire. The whirr of the President's US Army helicopter caught the Edensor villagers by surprise and they rushed from their homes in shirt-sleeves and carpet slippers to join a posse of security men waiting for the touchdown in a field at the back of the churchyard.

After visiting Ireland, JFK had flown to RAF Waddington in Lincolnshire and then made a private hour-long pilgrimage from there to Edensor. He walked from a field over the deer leap on a specially-constructed bridge that the estate workmen had put up. For a brief moment he forgot all his troubles to stand in the quiet Derbyshire churchyard beside the grave of his sister, Kathleen Devonshire who was killed on May 13, 1948, when the 10-seater private jet she was travelling in, while on her way to the South of France with a close friend, crashed in stormy weather.

After visiting his sister's grave, JFK walked the 100 yards through the churchyard to where cars were waiting. Then, as he stepped into the car, the crowd of around 25 reacted with a flutter of restrained applause. JFK stood back, smiled, waved and ducked back into the Bentley. Within minutes of driving through the grounds to Chatsworth House, he was airborne again and on his way back to RAF Waddington. From there, Air Force One whisked him to Gatwick, were he was received by Prime Minister Harold McMillan.

Most of Waddington's personnel were unaware of the President's visit until after the event, when the news spread like wildfire throughout the camp. I was probably spending the day in Lincoln with Pam and didn't know anything about it until I returned to Vulcan block that evening. Then I learned that during the visit, security at the camp had been tighter than it was at any other time. No one was allowed in or out and RAF Police with dogs patrolled the entire perimeter. However, residents of Married Quarters quickly found out what was going on and were on hand, albeit at a safe distance, to wave to Mr. Kennedy on his return from Edensor.

It might be asked, why Waddington? RAF Finningley was much closer to the quaint village of Edensor and, being a V-bomber station, could have been made just as secure as Waddington. My guess is that it was because the visit occurred during the weekend, when most stations were manned by skeleton staffs, even alert-conscious V-bomber stations. But Waddington was the Master Diversion airfield for a wide swathe of the surrounding country and where the control tower was permanently manned and the runway 'live' 24 hours a day, 7 days a week. So it made sense for the white, silver and blue Boeing 707, which was 'Air Force One' during Kennedy's presidency, to land surreptitiously at Waddington, where its scheduled arrival was a closely guarded secret.

Sadly, JFK himself had only four more months left to live before he too would be interred, but no one could have known that at the time.

Air Force One during John F. Kennedy's presidency

Chapter 15: Ground Movements

Just as it was on 230 OCU at Finningley, part of the job on The Line was to be a member of starter and seeing-in ground crews. The starter crew duties were much the same as on the OCU, the only exception being that the B1A Vulcan start system employed an electric starter motor, so there was no Palouste. Otherwise, all was the same. 'Seeing an aircraft in' is the phrase used to guide a Vulcan (or any other aircraft for that matter) to its parking space, put wheel chocks in place, apply ground power and then do a post-flight inspection relevant to one's trade.

The prevailing wind at Waddington generally blew across the airfield from a southerly direction, which meant that aircraft took off and landed on runway 21 (see map on page 41), ending up at the 03 end of the runway. At the risk of 'teaching my grandmother how to suck eggs', airfield runway numbers reflect the magnetic compass heading along which they are laid out, so that 21 is actually on a heading of 210 degrees and 03 is the 30 degree heading in the reciprocal or opposite direction (030).

(Interestingly, because the earth's magnetic pole wanders around over time, the current runway headings at Waddington are 20 and 02).

Coming off the 03 end of the runway placed a newly-landed Vulcan neatly in the vicinity of the E and D dispersals. A marshaller, equipped with a pair of large yellow or Day-Glo 'bats', would be positioned on the perimeter taxiway, at the entrance to whichever of these dispersals the Vulcan was to be guided. Another marshaller would be positioned at the appropriate intersection within the dispersal complex to guide the aircraft in the direction, left or right, to access the appropriate pan. At that point, the Crew Chief would step forward and plug in his long-lead. He would then 'talk' the pilot into the pan, advising him when to stop. Ground crew members would then haul the chocks into place and plug in the ground power cables before switching ground electrical power on to the aircraft. The rest was up to the aircrew to shut down the engines and deplane, helped by the Crew Chief, who would have opened the cabin access door by this time. A crew coach would have already arrived by the time the crew climbed out and fuel bowsers would soon arrive to be available for refuelling the aircraft. It was the same drill for an aircraft destined for C dispersal, except that it would have a longer trip along the taxiway to that dispersal entrance.

Marshalling during daylight was fairly easy, although a bit intimidating the first few times one experienced it with a Vulcan because of the size of the approaching aircraft. All one had to do was keep an eye on the nose-wheel and make sure it stayed on the yellow line painted along the centreline of the taxiway. The line separated at the entrance to the dispersal; one part kept on going along the centre of the main taxiway, but a spur peeled off, curving into the entrance of each dispersal and similarly spurred off at the intersections within the dispersal complex. The marshaller, using standard NATO marshalling signals, guided the pilot through the first turn. One bat was held stationary and pointed at a 45 degree angle to the ground to indicate which direction the aircraft needed to turn. The other bat continued to be waved up and down to indicate 'continue to proceed'. Just before the point where the pilot was about to lose sight of him, the marshaller brought his non-stationary arm and bat to join the one that was stationary, holding both arms together horizontally, such that he was pointing with both bats towards the next marshaller. He then gave a salute with one bat to let the pilot know that this particular marshaller was finished. The process was then repeated by the next marshaller, all the way to the pan threshold, where the Crew Chief was able to plug in his long lead and micromanage the pilot the remainder of the way, making sure the twin wheels that constituted the nose wheel came to a stop when the picketing lug, just forward of the wheels, was over a thick steel ring recessed in the concrete that could be used to 'picket' the Vulcan in place, should the weather or other considerations make it necessary.

Picketing is the name given to the act of anchoring an aircraft to something very heavy or completely immovable, usually to prevent interaction with high winds. In the Vulcan's case, it also prevented it from tipping tailwards in unusual circumstances. The method of picketing a Vulcan was to position it so that a horizontal, cylindrical, picketing lug at the lower end of the nose wheel leg, positioned between the two wheels that formed the nose wheel, was directly above a sturdy steel ring buried in the concrete of the pan with its upper half accessible within a shallow recess in the concrete. One end of a hefty, adjustable, double-ended hook device was hooked over the nose wheel picketing lug, while the other end was hooked to the steel ring. A screw jack on the device was then tightened up to anchor the Vulcan firmly to the pan. Typically, it was the Crew Chief's responsibility to apply the picket, or to supervise its installation.

Marshalling a Vulcan at night was a much different scenario than it was during daylight. Instead of bats, the marshaller would be equipped with lighted wands. But now he would be confronted by a pair of bright landing lamps, in the taxiing position, pointed directly at him, essentially blinding him. Instead of a yellow line, he had to somehow keep the aircraft centred on a series of green taxiway lights set along the length of the centreline. My first time to do this was one of the

Picketing lug (ringed)

scariest experiences I have ever had, positioned out on the taxiway at the entrance to C dispersal, seeing this huge beast with flashing anti-collision lights and two great glaring landing lamps coming towards me. Even though they were in the 'taxi' position, they were still very bright and dazzled me to the extent that I was not able to see very much. Fortunately, as the Vulcan got near, the pilot seemed to realize what effect the lamps were having on me, because he retracted them. Only then could I see where the nose-wheel was in relation to the glowing green taxiway lights that marked the centreline and was able to signal the pilot to turn at the right place.

***

A Vulcan moving under its own steam, if you'll pardon the expression, was one thing. Its motive power was under the control of a pilot and a ground crew's job was the relatively easy task of waving marshalling bats or wands, depending on the time of day or night. Moving a Vulcan on the ground, without assistance from either pilot or running engines, required the services of a Tugmaster, generally referred to as a Tug, which was a large, powerful type of tractor that only a few MT (Mechanical Transport) drivers were qualified to operate.

The tow bar that connected the Tug to a Vulcan was a huge piece of ground equipment, as might be imagined when considering what it was required to tow. Over most of its length it was in the form of four parallel lengths of hefty tubular steel in a square box configuration. A tubular steel lattice tied the four main members together. At the Tug end, a long shock absorber set within the box structure terminated at the towing end in a large, horizontal steel ring that hooked onto the Tug. At the Vulcan end, the four tubular steel members of the box structure narrowed down to a single point that terminated in a lug. This mated with a fixture at the midpoint of the aircraft's nose wheel leg.

A swing down frame from the main structure also connected the tow bar to the nose wheel hub. The hub was actually a tube through which a bar was passed to mate it with two lugs on the swing down frame. Two small wheels on the bottom of the swing down frame provided support for the aircraft end of the tow bar. A similar set of wheels on the bottom of another sub-frame provided support at the Tug end, thus allowing the tow bar to be wheeled around and positioned, independently of the Tug. The entire contraption was painted in beautiful Ground Equipment Blue, which was all the rage in the Cold War days, although the colour may have been changed later to a more visible yellow, but that was after my time in the service.

The tow bar was a minor engineering marvel, designed so that it could be hitched up to a Tug and a Vulcan by one man, namely the driver. This was accomplished by two manually operated screw jacks incorporated on the tow bar, by which its height could be raised or lowered. One screw jack raised and lowered the swing down frame, which in turn, adjusted the height of the lug that connected with the nose wheel leg. The other screw jack adjusted the angle of the frame on which the Tug-end wheels were mounted to raise or lower the tow ring to the height of the hitching point. If this all sounds complicated, the illustrations below and on the following page might make it a little clearer.

In practice, however, Tug drivers were temperamentally disinclined to mess around with the slow process of operating screw jacks and aligning the hitching points by themselves. So what it came down to was a team effort that required the muscle power of three or four ground crew members to lift the tow bar into position so that the attachments to both the nose wheel and the Tug ends could be made in short order. Besides, a Tug driver would not be moving a Vulcan by himself because it needed at least one other man to sit in the pilot's seat to operate the aircraft's brakes, should the need arise.

Another view of the tow bar from the tug end.

Chapter 16: The KGB and Friends

Because the V-Force was Britain's nuclear deterrent during the Cold War, it was understandably a target of USSR espionage and sabotage, as were those of us who were members of the force. Therefore, we were constantly warned to be on the alert for security risks and Russian attempts to compromise us in any number of ways that might lead us into betraying our country.

Understandably, security at V-bomber bases was tight, to say the least. The aircraft were dispersed around the airfield on individual concrete pans. The pans were usually grouped in fours and the set of four generally referred to as a 'dispersal', because the object was to scatter the aircraft around the airfield so that they would be less of an easy target during a conventional bombing or strafing attack. (The 230 OCU Vulcan B2 dispersal at Finningley was an exception, however; five pans were arrayed in an arc in front of the OCU hangar).

During the hours of darkness, each aircraft was illuminated by a ring of sodium floodlights placed around its pan based on the theory that anyone entering the circle of light, intent on approaching an aircraft, would stand out like a sore thumb in the yellow glare of the lights. Armed RAF Police dog handlers with their Alsatian dogs restrained on quick-release leashes patrolled the areas around the aircraft. It was not uncommon for those of us who worked on the aircraft to be challenged by a dog handler and asked to prove our identity. On more than one occasion, I was stopped by a dog handler when I entered into the ring of lights around a pan. They first demanded to know who I was and then, when I had verbally identified myself, was ordered to remove my security badge, place it face up on the ground and then step back several paces – we were all required to wear a security badge that contained our photograph with rank and name. When I had complied with this command, the dog handler would then came forward to examine the badge while his mean-looking Alsatian kept a beady eye on me, no doubt savouring the thought of chomping on my arm, or some other appendage, should I turn out to be a saboteur or Soviet spy.

***

Once, at Finningley while I was in a Vulcan crew compartment doing some work, a radar fitter was performing some checks on the NBS (Navigation Bombing System) which employed a powerful radar system that he was operating in a live condition. The huge scanner housed in the nose of the Vulcan was emitting radar frequency sweeps of the surrounding area. Suddenly, an SNCO raced up the ladder into the compartment and hastily told the radar fitter to shut the system down. He went on to say that the Line office had been notified that 'a big black car with CD plates' had been observed driving up and down the nearby A1. The Russians were apparently doing a little electronic espionage that day.

It seems they were also interested in the historic city of Lincoln, or maybe not so much the city itself. Some time after my departure from Waddington, Geoff Supple was transferred from the Flight Line Squadron to the Supplementary Storage Area (SSA) – a large compound directly across the A15 Lincoln-to-Sleaford road from Bravo Dispersal, where the Nuclear Weapons were stored. While there, he was briefed that members of the Russian embassy were known to apply to the Home Office for a travel permit to go on a 'cultural' visit to Lincoln, the day prior to the klaxon announcing a Mickey Finn dispersal exercise. These exercises were always on a 'surprise' basis and no one at the station level was aware of when they would occur. So it would appear that the KGB had infiltrated the very heart of Bomber Command and knew what was going on before we did. It isn't known if they ever made it to the historic cathedral area of the city or its many Roman archaeological sites, but they were definitely observed on the A15 during the preliminary part of the exercise, no doubt taking note of all the activity at the SSA.

***

On another occasion, in 1963, the CND (Campaign for Nuclear Disarmament) let it be known far and wide that it was organizing a major protest demonstration at Easter with planned marches on installations related to nuclear weapons. It was well known that there was active Communist Party involvement in these kinds of demonstrations with tacit encouragement and possible funding by the USSR. The British government didn't know exactly where the demonstrations would take place and so issued a directive to increase security at all possible targets, including V-bomber stations. When our shift arrived at E dispersal to start work that day, we were immediately corralled together in the crew room for a briefing. Our junior engineering officer explained that there was a possibility that demonstrators might attempt to gain access to the aircraft dispersal areas from the adjacent open land and it was our job to assist the RAF police in preventing this from happening. The open land was basically grassy fields and the only barrier between it and the dispersals was a low perimeter fence.

"You will be stationed at regular intervals along the length of the fence," the officer began. "If any demonstrators climb over the fence, you are to politely and gently assist them back to the other side. Do not, I repeat, do not harm anyone but treat them with kid gloves. However, if anyone manages to reach one of the pans and as much as lays a finger on an aircraft, or any item of ground equipment – that is considered to be an act of sabotage and, in such a circumstance, you can do whatever you like to them."

As it turned out, the demonstrators never came anywhere near Waddington. They marched to the Atomic Weapons Research Establishment (AWRE) at Aldermaston instead, so we were spared from having to 'help' anyone return to the other side of the perimeter fence.

**

The Russians did manage to compromise some individuals, but not, as far as I am aware, at Waddington. It became known, however, that a SNCO at nearby RAF Digby, a Chief Technician ironically named Douglas Britten had provided them with photographs of sensitive intelligence information that he had access to in his work in Signals Intelligence. It began in 1962, when he was approached by a Russian intelligence officer who persuaded to provide him with a certain type of wireless transmitter. Britten knew that that particular transmitter model was obsolete in the RAF and could be obtained very easily on the open market, so he probably saw no harm in providing one; that and the fact that the Russians would pay him handsomely for it was a big enough lure. Later, when offered more cash for another seemingly innocuous hand-over, the crafty Russians secretly photographed him as he accepted the cash – and the trap was sprung. They then provided him with a device that James Bond would have been proud of; it was a clever camera disguised as a leather wallet that could copy documents just by rolling the edge of the wallet over them. Britten then began copying sensitive intelligence documents that he had access to due to the nature of his work. He would then hand the information over to his 'handler' at pre-arranged meetings that were artfully mapped out to detect any surveillance by our side. Britten's big blunder and the reason he got caught was that he was photographed by an MI5 operative as he hand-delivered a message to a Russian Consulate office because his 'handler' had failed to turn up for an arranged meeting. He was sentenced to 25 years in prison at the Old Bailey in 1968.

This all came to our attention on the V-force when the code names for the entire radar and ECM devices were abruptly changed. These code names were 'colourful' in that they were all of a two-word nature assigned from the 'Rainbow Code'. The first word of the code name was that of a random colour and the second word was some completely random noun. Everyone even remotely involved with the equipment never used its real name but referred to it by its code name. This just became second nature and was supposed to prevent eavesdroppers and such like from knowing what the real name of the equipment was if they happened to overhear it in conversation or read something that referred to it. An example of this was the Doppler radar that measured the Vulcan's groundspeed. I don't believe it will contravene the Official Secrets Act after all these years if I reveal that its code name was *Green Satin,* but following Britten's betrayal, it was changed to something else. The reason we knew about this is because we were briefed on the betrayal, which was given as the explanation for why the code names had been changed and also as a reminder on how not fall victim of this type of espionage.

The Rainbow Code was actually a hangover from the Second World War during which British intelligence discovered that, thanks to the German penchant for efficient organization, information relating to their secret equipment could be deduced simply by inferring from the equipment's code name. Learning from this mistake, the British invented a completely random system for assigning code names to sensitive equipment that gave no hint to its intended purpose, while still being easy to remember. The 'Rainbow Code' was supposedly used only up until 1958, but was still used on V-bombers up until 1968, when it was learned from Doug Britten's interrogation that a list of the code names and the equipment to which they referred had been handed over to the Russians.

Chapter 17: QRA at Waddington

While the majority of the V-Force aircraft were used in a continuous training role – bombing accuracy, simulated in the case of nuclear weapons and actual live dropping of conventional high explosive bombs, navigation exercises, emergency drills and general familiarity with the aircraft – they never ever flew with live nuclear weapons on board. However, a small number of aircraft on each station were 'loaded for bear'. The bear, in this case, was the USSR. Each squadron in Bomber Command supplied a crew to man a V-bomber armed with a live nuclear weapon. Crews and aircraft were kept at a minimum of 15 minute readiness to scramble in the event of an impending attack by the Russians. For this purpose these nuclear armed V-bombers were stationed on a dedicated dispersal at each station, with their dedicated aircrews and ground crews. This continuous state of readiness was known as the Quick Reaction Alert or QRA in everyday parlance. Since there were three squadrons based at Waddington, we had three Vulcans on QRA, located on Alpha dispersal, which was nearest to the runway 21 threshold – this being the operational runway because of the prevailing wind. It was also near the Operations block, where the duty aircrew remained on standby.

Being on QRA was both a skive and a pain in the rear for all concerned. Ground crew QRA duty lasted for one week, being performed by personnel delegated from the 'A' and 'B' shifts of the Line Squadron, nine from each shift (three men per aircraft). During that time, the first shift would be on duty for 24 hours, commencing at 08:00 hours on Monday, during which they were confined to the QRA dispersal area for the entire time, except for meal breaks. In the normal course of a day, there was very little work to be done because the aircraft were locked and were theoretically ready for take off within 2 minutes. Therefore, they were serviceable and required no maintenance. Bomber Command did not tolerate major unserviceability problems on QRA aircraft. If a fault occurred that could not be rectified within the space of one hour, during which time the aircraft was temporarily stood down from QRA, the afflicted aircraft would be taken off QRA and replaced with one that was serviceable. This was a major headache for all concerned, because it meant disarming the faulty aircraft and arming its replacement.

The ground crew stayed mostly in the crew room and passed the time in whatever way they could. Some watched television, some read books or magazines, while others played cards or darts. This was interspersed with general tasks that the SNCO in charge of QRA, or one of the aircraft Crew Chiefs, might assign. Sleeping accommodation consisted of a number of long, olive-coloured caravans that were partitioned into compartments each containing two bunk-beds. Usually, there were enough compartments available that each man could have one to himself. The approximately 6 foot by 8 foot compartment was very basic, consisting of the two bunk-beds against one wall on each of which rested a mattress encased in heavy vinyl. There was some limited space provided in the room for personal belongings, but the upper bunk was handy for dumping whatever kit a person had with them. A clean set of blankets, sheets and pillows was issued to each man from a store at the dispersal office building, at the beginning of his duty.

At 08:00 hours on Tuesday morning, the first shift was relieved by the second shift, which then remained on the site for the next 24 hours, while the first shift stood down and was free from duty for that whole day. Then, on Wednesday morning, the first shift relieved the second shift and so it went on for the remainder of the working week. At the weekend, the second shift stayed on duty for both Saturday and Sunday and was relieved on Monday morning by the new first shift. If this seems unfair, it needs to be explained that the first shift was always assigned to those who would have been working night shift had they been on the Line and vice versa for the second shift. Therefore, any given individual who was from that week's night shift when on QRA would be from the day shift the next time he was detailed for QRA duty. The scheduling of the shifts was arranged in such a way that the weekend crew would be on night shift on their return to the Line and so were able to take a few hours off to relax and catch up with their normal lives before resuming their normal duties back on the Line. This system ensured that all duty periods were evenly shared by both shifts.

Although the ground crews had little to do, they were on standby for alerts at all times, either the real thing – an imminent attack by the Russians, or, more realistically, a practice 'Alert'. I've heard there's a saying attributed to wartime Lancaster aircrew that described flying on bombing raids as long hours of boredom interspersed with moments of sheer, stark terror. QRA was a little like that, except that the 'sheer, stark terror' part needs to be substituted with 'adrenaline-fuelled bursts of activity'.

The adrenaline rush was brought on by the obnoxious sound of a klaxon being broadcast over the station Tannoy system. After a few seconds of klaxon exposure, it ceased and a voice intoned *"Exercise Edom! Exercise Edom! Readiness state zero five. I repeat, readiness state zero five"* The message was broadcast directly from Bomber Command HQ at High Wycombe and could issue forth at any hour of the day or night, although only at the QRA site during the 'quiet hours', when normal humanity was deep in the bosom of sleep. To those of us on QRA duty, however, the klaxon's effect would either cause us to instantly drop whatever we were doing, if it sounded during normal waking time, or be brought instantly and rudely awake if it happened in the middle of the night, whereupon we would immediately leap out of bed. No period of a week's duty on QRA passed without a number of nocturnal alerts, both during week nights and at weekends. Of course, we had our fair share of daylight alerts as well. Two days would not pass without an Exercise Edom – and a weekend alert was always a sure bet.

During a daytime alert, we just raced out to our assigned aircraft, ready to assist the Crew Chief in any way he directed, while we awaited the aircrew's arrival. The crew entrance doors of the QRA aircraft were normally kept locked and theoretically, only the captain had the key. But the lock was a very simple type used on the motorcars of that era, so all of the Crew Chiefs had obtained copies from the local Halfords. Therefore, by the time the aircrew screeched to a halt in their beat up aircrew bus, the door on each aircraft was already open and the access ladder in place, ready for them to climb aboard.

Most systems on QRA aircraft were kept continuously powered up from a ground power unit that ran constantly. Therefore, there was not much for them to do except start the power flying controls (PFCs) and check a few of the already powered up systems. This readiness condition meant that the aircraft could be launched within 5 minutes of an alert being received. The engines were not started at this 5-minute readiness alert stage, but if the Bomber Controller raised the alert level to that of 2 minutes readiness, which sometimes happened, then the engines were started and the main wheel chocks dragged to the edge of the pan, out of the way.

Unlike B2 Vulcan, the B1A start system was equipped with an electric motor start system on each engine. Therefore, instead of the B2's pneumatic start, initiated with bleed air from its AAPP, the B1A rapid start was achieved by using a massive 'Simstart' cart. There were four Simstart cables that snaked out from the cart, one for each engine. They were plugged into two receptacles in each of the main undercarriage bays; two sets for the starboard engines and two for the port side engines. These cables connected a 96 volts DC supply from the Simstart cart directly to each engine's electric starter motor, bypassing the normal, on-board engine start system. The Simstart cart was an array of heavy duty batteries arranged in four sets of 96 volts DC – one set for each of the Vulcan's engines. Each set of batteries had its own dedicated, cart-mounted, engine starting panel that was identical to the starter system on board the aircraft. In essence, the Simstart cart comprised four complete and separate engine starting systems, all under the control of the Crew Chief, who could initiate the start sequences by pushing the four start buttons on the trolley's control console. In a scramble situation, he would push all four buttons in rapid succession, thus initiating a simultaneous start of all four engines.

On receiving a change of alert status from Bomber Command to go from 5 minutes to 2 minutes readiness, the captain would give the 'start engines' order to the Crew Chief, who would then react by pushing all four buttons on the Simstart cart, causing all of the engines to start simultaneously and come up to idling speed. At that point, it only needed the appropriate command and code word from Bomber Command for our three Vulcans, together with the QRA aircraft on the

The ground crew in the act of plugging the Simstart cables into the port and starboard undercarriage bays.

British Pathe documentary 'Scramble in 2 minutes (1960), courtesy of Youtube.

In the foreground; the Crew Chief operates the engine start buttons on the Simstart trolley.

In the background; one of the ground crew stands ready to disconnect the starboard Simstart cables on the Crew Chief's signal.

British Pathe documentary 'Scramble in 2 minutes (1960), courtesy of Youtube.

other V-bomber stations, to get airborne within the 2 minute window and be on their long, one-way trip to Russia. Happily it never came to that, but occasionally the command would be given for the aircraft to taxi. This was as close as it got to an actual take off. At the 'taxi' command, the Crew Chief, in contact with the pilot through his long lead, motioned for us to pull out the Simstart cables, then the power cables and finally the nose wheel chock. We pulled everything clear and knew to get clear of the pan very quickly ourselves because the aircraft was about to leave there in a hurry.

Usually, the three Vulcans taxied out of the dispersal carefully, then went onto the runway and taxied its full length before returning to their QRA dispersal pan. There was one particular night-time alert, however, that is burned into my memory. The order to taxi came down from Command, whereupon we performed our tasks before quickly taking cover from the jet blast. The pilot of the Vulcan to which I was assigned seemed to get carried away with the drama of the moment because, instead of taxiing out at low engine rpm until he was clear of the pan, he rammed the throttles open as soon as he was given the 'all-clear' from the Crew Chief and kept them open the whole time. It's just as well that we ground crew members had taken cover because the situation soon became very hairy. The heavy Simstart cables and the main ground power cables began whipping around in the powerful jet blast like huge serpents in a horror film. Worst of all were the large wheel chocks, triangular in shape, around 6 feet in length, made of solid inch-thick wood and shod with sturdy steel strips on their bottom outer edges. They were so heavy that a grown man couldn't lift one clear of the ground by himself, yet the huge chocks cart-wheeled end over end across the pan as though they were just matchsticks. Showers of sparks sprang up every time one of the steel edge strips struck the pan's concrete surface. Any unfortunate airman caught in their path would have been killed or, at best, severely injured. The ground power unit also took off on a long trip across the pan, heavy though it was, but fortunately was undamaged.

The three nuclear-armed Vulcans taxied the length of the runway and then returned back to the dispersal along the perimeter taxiway. When the crew of my team's Vulcan deplaned, the Crew

Chief, who also had to quickly dive for cover during the Vulcan's wild departure, had an angry word or two with the aircraft captain. The captain apologized and nothing more was said after that.

The only times we were permitted to leave the vicinity of the QRA site was to take our meals in the Airmen's Mess, but on the basis that only one man from each crew could be released at a time. We had a beat-up old Land Rover – an ancient model unlike any other Land Rover on the station. The only thing that made it special was the large Day-Glo letters spelling out 'QRA' affixed to both doors. We had one concession at the Mess – our own exclusive parking space right outside the main entrance so that we could return to the dispersal rapidly if an alert occurred while we were having our meal. And it frequently did. When the klaxon sounded, we just left our food on the table and made a dash for the Land Rover. It didn't have any fancy flashing lights or a siren, but the arm on which the horn button was mounted could be swivelled around to the passenger side so that whoever sat in that seat was able to keep his hand on the horn to blare out a warning all the way back to the dispersal. In the meantime, those remaining on QRA filled in for the absence of their crew members until the missing men returned to their assigned Vulcans.

On one occasion, the airman driving the Land Rover back from the Mess in response to an alert took the corner from the roadway into the dispersal office building area a little too quickly, causing the vehicle to tip over onto its side. No one was injured, so they all just jumped out and ran to their aircraft as though nothing had happened. Unfortunately, the Land Rover received only superficial injury, so we couldn't have it exchanged for a more recent model.

The airman who turned over the Land Rover was a bit of a strange lad. He was smart, in a boffin kind of way, but a little lacking in the 'street smart' department. That week was his first time on QRA and also his first call out in the wee small hours. As luck would have it, he was on my crew. As usual, on suddenly being awakened in the middle of the night by the sound of the klaxon, we just threw on some trousers and an anorak over our pyjamas, crammed our boots on to our bare feet and raced out to our assigned aircraft. All of us, that is, except our new lad.

"Where the hell's D---?" Someone shouted.

No one knew, but we took up our positions and hoped he would turn up. He did, but it was several minutes later. There he was, strolling out to the pan, wearing full uniform including his tie knotted and in place, shoes laced up and his beret on his head. The Crew Chief almost suffered a fit when he witnessed this and promptly collared D to utter a stream of unprintable words into his shell-like ear-hole.

Chapter 18: Wheels up on the Runway

Waddington's airfield was open and its control tower manned 24 hours a day, 7 days a week because it was a Master Diversion airfield in those days. This meant that if a military aircraft (or civilian for that matter) could not make it to their home or destination airfield due to weather or an emergency situation, Waddington was open and able to receive them. One of the airfield's significant features was a massive cage-like neon-tube beacon, in the shape of a truncated cone, mounted atop the station water tower that continuously flashed the letters WA in red neon bursts of Morse code, making it stand out in the night-time sky from the many other airfields in the surrounding Lincolnshire countryside and easily recognizable to the crew of any aircraft being diverted there.

Because the control tower was always manned, many different aircraft made practice approaches and touch-and-go 'rollers' on the main runway, day and night. In addition, the nearby RAF College Cranwell used the runway in a similar manner to help train its student pilots. These touch-and-goes were such a frequent occurrence that we of the ground crew became oblivious to the small, relatively quiet Jet Provosts performing landings and take-offs while we worked. Then late one night, all hands were called on deck, so to speak. We were told that an aircraft had made a wheels-up landing on the main runway and everyone on duty was being mustered to help get it off. All of our previously airborne Vulcans had already returned to base, except one which still needed to be recovered.

Within minutes, an assortment of vehicles, loaded with Line personnel, was heading along the runway to where the hapless aircraft sat forlornly on its belly. As soon as I got there, I could see that it was a Jet Provost and because it bore a distinctive broad, light blue band around the aft section of its fuselage, knew that it was from the RAF College Cranwell. The area surrounding the JP was awash with people from the Aircraft Servicing Flight (ASF), fire fighting vehicles, engineering officers and Uncle Tom Cobley and all; it was one of those situations where there are too many Chiefs and not enough Indians. Various people were trying to make their voices heard above others in

One of the Royal Air Force College Cranwell's Jet Provosts as signified by the blue band around its fuselage.

offering suggestions in what to do. In the midst of all this, the student and instructor were trying to climb out of the cockpit. The fire service vehicles soon trained spot lights on the aircraft and someone produced a step ladder that enabled the two occupants to descend to the ground, after taking the necessary action to render the ejection seats safe.

The student was, of course, a Cranwell cadet who was visibly trembling, maybe as much from the cool night air as from his very recent experience. The instructor was a Master Pilot, who looked very pale and extremely downcast.

I overheard the Master Pilot say, to no one in particular, "If only that bloody hump hadn't been there!" From this, I gathered that he had suddenly become aware of the impending situation and had increased power to get out of it, but the JP's underside encountered 'The Hump' on the Waddington runway before he could gain sufficient height to clear it.

The Waddington runway is not flat and level. Its surface rises gradually into a hump part way along its length, before descending just as gradually on the other side. You might be tempted to ask, why is there a hump? My suspicion is that it's because the Waddington airfield sits athwart Ermine Street, the ancient Roman road that connected Lindum Colonia, the Roman name from which Lincoln is derived, to that other well known Roman colony of Londinium – no prizes for guessing the identity of the modern-day city to which that refers. The road's ancient route passes diagonally across Waddington's main runway, which leads me to surmise that the hump may be due to land settlement on either side of the Roman road's ancient but solid foundation, resulting in the rise in the local topography. Interestingly, it's a little known fact that the central taxiway of Echo dispersal lies along and on top of a small length of the original Roman road. Getting back to the story; the hydraulic jacks were wrong for the job. They just wouldn't fit under the Jet Provost. Meanwhile, the firemen brought inflatable bladders to put under the wings in an attempt to raise the JP so that its wheels could be lowered. In the midst of all this, the Station Commander showed up.

Group Captain 'Cyclops' Brown wasn't in a very good mood. He had been enjoying the camaraderie of his fellow officers at a dining-in evening in the Officers' Mess when news came that the Jet Provost was sitting on *his* runway with its wheels neatly folded into its wheel bays instead of being in contact with the runway, where they should have been. He immediately demanded that someone drive him to the scene of the crime and on arriving there, resplendent in his mess dress complete with miniature wartime medals, swayed slightly from the effects of his very recent liquid fortification as he approached the activity surrounding the stricken aircraft. The group of people around the plane parted like the waters of Red Sea to let him pass.

"Where's the pilot?" He demanded, as soon as he got within touching range of the Jet Provost.

The Master Pilot instructor shuffled sheepishly forward, coming face to face with the one-eyed Group Captain, famous for the black pirate-like eye patch he wore in place of the eye he had lost while engaged with a Luftwaffe Dornier during Second World War. The cadet student, meanwhile, hung back, trying to blend into the background. Cyclops then proceeded to give the Master Pilot a severe bollocking in front of everyone present, before taking charge of the situation.

While this was going on, it became obvious that the inflatable bladders weren't able to raise the Jet Provost high enough to lower its wheels. Maybe it was Cyclops himself, or perhaps someone else, but it was then suggested that even though the wheels couldn't be lowered, as things stood, the wings were now high enough to allow space for a few strong people to crawl underneath and bodily lift the aircraft higher. There were certainly enough of us young, strong Line 'animals' (a nickname we didn't particularly care for) to get underneath the wings for the plan to work. Volunteers were called for with a more than adequate response forthcoming. With this now considered the way forward, the Master Pilot climbed back into the cockpit and then as many of us as could fit, crammed ourselves under the wings with our knees bent and backs up against the underside of the wings.

On the given word, we started straightening our knees while pushing up with our backs against the wings. The Jet Provost lifted easily and it didn't take long before we had the aircraft high enough for the pilot to push the undercarriage 'down' button. He then manually pumped the wheels down until they locked and was rewarded with 'three greens' in confirmation. We human jacks then allowed the plane to settle down on its wheels and were then able to step out from under the wings. The next phase in the operation was for all of us to line up against the leading edges of both wings and push the Jet Provost backwards all the way into the nearest hangar. It remained there for several days, until a 'Queen Mary' aircraft ground transporter arrived to carry it back to Cranwell or perhaps to a Maintenance Unit for substantial repairs.

The pilot and student's fates are unknown. It probably didn't earn the student too many Brownie points, landing without properly performing one of the most important items on his landing checklist. As for the instructor, who may have been dozing or otherwise distracted by the boring repetition of the landings and take offs, it probably meant the end of his tour as a flight instructor. Our airborne Vulcan, meanwhile, had been diverted to RAF Coningsby, so we no longer needed to worry about it.

Chapter 19: Detachment to RAF Coningsby

During the summer of 1963, it was announced that operations were to be temporarily transferred to RAF Coningsby while the runway at Waddington was being resurfaced. Those of us who were single were to be accommodated at Coningsby, which made a few of us unhappy because it separated us from our Lincoln girlfriends. One of the lads, Geoff Sykes, had a car and intended to drive back to Waddington each evening at the cessation of work. (Operations were only being carried out during daylight hours for the duration of the Waddington shutdown). Geoff let it be known that he was willing to take passengers of a similar frame of mind in exchange for sharing the petrol costs. I, for one, jumped at the opportunity, as did Al Hewitt and one other, whose name I don't remember.

It worked out well. Each evening we set off from Coningsby on the 23 mile drive back to our Waddington 'home' in Vulcan block, where we showered and changed into civilian clothes before going into Lincoln to be with our beloveds. Early next morning we would do the reverse, leaving early enough to be able to get back to Coningsby in time to start work at the appointed hour.

Our seating selection in Geoff's Austin A50 Cambridge car was random, but once chosen on the first day, we seemed to stick with the same seating plan. Mine was the rear left seat of the four-door car. This was to be significant.

The detachment wasn't for too many days; probably two weeks at the most and so by the second week, our routine was well established. We left Coningsby on the A153 road towards Sleaford, but then turned north at Billinghay and took the smaller B1189 as the first of a series of small country roads that eventually got us back to Waddington. The problem with those country roads was that right-of-way, when one crosses the other, was not always clearly marked. On one of our last trips, we were travelling along at a reasonable speed, approaching a crossroads. Gazing out of my window, I noticed another car on the road that intersected with ours. It was heading towards the same crossroads. As I watched, it disappeared from view behind a tall

Typical Austin A50 Cambridge of the era.

hedgerow that bordered that road. It casually occurred to me that the
other car was likely to arrive at the crossroads about the same time as
our car and I hoped that one of us would see the other and stop.
Moments later, we were at the crossroads. I was looking in the
direction from which the other car would be approaching, thinking it
would not have arrived there yet, but to my horror it came into view
just feet from where I sat and was not slowing down, let alone stopping.
It crashed into our car just behind where I sat. I have no recollection of
exactly what happened next, except that I remember rolling over and
over along what I thought was the road, unable to stop myself and
wondering if this was 'It'. I could feel my face in contact with the
ground at various moments so it also came to mind that if I survived,
my face would be a terrible mess. After what seemed to be an eternity,
I finally stopped tumbling and lay there for a time until my breath
caught up with the rest of me. First of all, I was thankful to still be
alive. Then I moved all my limbs and was thankful again that they all
seemed to be in working order, except that one knee felt painful. This
all happened in less time than it takes to tell it and so the next thing I

did was lift up my head to see where I was and what had happened to the others. I was surprised to see that I was on the grass verge and not on the road surface as I had feared, while tumbling. The next thing I saw was Geoff's car upside down in the middle of the road. Al Hewitt and the other chap were still inside the car, on the roof, which was now the floor and looking bewilderedly out of the rear window. A strange thought that immediately jumped into my mind was that they looked just like two goldfish in a bowl.

Another Waddington airman, who happened to be driving his own car and had not been too far ahead of us, looked in his rear view mirror, expecting to see our car behind him as before. Instead, he saw the car now suddenly upside down in the middle of the road. He immediately turned around and came racing back to assist. Meanwhile, the car that collided with us, which by coincidence was also being driven by an RAF serviceman from Digby, had ended up nose into a hedge on the opposite side of the crossroad intersection. By the time the assisting Waddington airman reached the crash site, I had managed to get up and was making my way to the upended car. Strangely, all of the doors were closed and to this day I do not know how I found myself tumbling along the grass verge when all of the others remained inside the car. It's relevant to mention that this was an era before seatbelts, otherwise we would have all been strapped in and I would probably have remained in the car. The Waddington airman and I opened the doors to allow Geoff, Al and the other man to extricate themselves. None of them were injured, although Al complained at having got a small piece of glass in his eye. My only injury was a swelling of my knee because of fluid that collected there due to it having received a hard blow. When we turned our attention to the other driver, it turned out that he was also uninjured.

With the help of some others who by this time had stopped, we got Geoff's car back on its wheels again. I vaguely remember getting a lift back to Waddington with the airman who turned back to assist and the next thing I remember of the incident was arriving at Pam's house in a mild state of shock. When she and her mum saw me, they immediately asked what had happened because, they said, I looked as though I had seen a ghost. Also, I think I had a few scratches on my face from being in contact with the grass verge. In retrospect, the worst injury was mental. Nowadays it has a name – PTSD, post traumatic stress disorder. For a long time afterwards, I was unable to ride as a passenger in anyone's car and would only travel by bus. Eventually, I was able to become a car passenger again, but it took a long time and even then, I became anxious if the car travelled at anything but a moderate speed.

That may have been the last day of our detachment to Coningsby because I don't remember going back there again.

Chapter 20: Engagements and Marriages

It seems that many of us on the squadron were of an age to settle down with one particular life partner. Pam and I got engaged in late August of 1963. Johnny Thorne, my scooter riding wingman also got engaged to Carol. Artie Milne got serious with his girlfriend Pauline and joined the ranks of the soon-to-be-married. Geoff Supple strayed a little from the Lincoln scene and found Joan in Grantham. He too put a shiny diamond ring on her finger around the same time. Meanwhile, Stan Eilbeck married Dorothy, his sweetheart from home, and brought her to Lincoln where they rented a cottage in the nearby hamlet of South Hykeham. We were introduced to her at a get-together at the Saracen's Head pub in Lincoln. (The pub itself was famous as a gathering place for Second World War squadron aircrew members, including those of the Dambusters, but was demolished and faded into history several years ago).

***

Because those of us newly-married couples were young and of lowly rank, none of us qualified for married quarters on the camp; we all had to find rented accommodation in the surrounding area. After much searching, Pam and I found a furnished flat on Mount Street in Lincoln. It was owned by a certain Mr. Brownlow. Mount Street was a fair distance from Waddington, but easily travelled on my trusty Lambretta. Our flat was the lower floor of a terraced house, while the upper floor was rented by another couple who seemed to keep themselves to themselves, so we never met them during the few months that we lived there.

There were some good things and some not so good things about our flat. The best thing, in my opinion, was the soft, downy, feather mattress on the double bed that a newly married couple could sink into. It was even nicer to crawl into and enjoy the warmth of my sleeping bride when I came home in the early hours of the morning, after finishing on night shift.

The worst thing about the flat was Mr. Brownlow's miserliness; a trait that would have put Scrooge to shame. Not content with the rent he charged, Brownlow had installed an electricity meter in the flat through which we were obliged to purchase the electricity we used. One shilling purchased a small quantity of electricity at the exorbitant rate to which he had calibrated the meter. To make matters worse, water in the flat was electrically heated, but the large copper hot water tank was completely bare, lacking insulation of any kind. We needed the hot water to bathe, wash our clothes and wash dishes, but any hot water remaining in the tank soon cooled down because it radiated out directly through the copper wall of the tank. We asked Brownlow to have the tank insulated, but he refused, although he came around every week to collect the rent and empty the meter. I put an ordinary blanket over it, but it did very little good. We stayed there for only four months, but more about that later.

***

Dorothy Eilbeck has some clear memories of those days, which she shared with me.

I remember inviting Johnny Thorne and Carol to tea at the cottage and they arrived on Johnny's Vespa scooter. Carol very scared because Johnny was still an L-rider and she shouldn't have been on the scooter. The meal was intended to include roast chicken, salad, bread and butter, dessert and cakes. Wedding present china was much in evidence. Towards the end of the meal Dorothy went to the kitchen for something and Stan followed her, remarking "What happened to the chicken?" Their first visitors – and a major part of the meal had been left in the kitchen!

Within three months of our marriage in 1964, my husband Stan – an RAF electrician - was posted to Labuan in Borneo from Waddington, near Lincoln. It was a one-year 'unaccompanied' tour, so we had to relinquish the little cottage we were renting and I returned home to my parents in Cumbria. Stan flew off to Borneo and seemed to enjoy his off-duty life in Labuan, which was on an island. He built a small catamaran with a friend and they spent many hours fishing in the tropical waters.

(Author's note: This was during the so-called Confrontation with President Sukarno of Indonesia who, unsatisfied with having to share half of the massive island of Borneo with Malaysia, was trying to take over the whole of it. Britain had a defence treaty with Malaysia, so we were supporting it in a major way in what was basically a shooting war.)

At last, the year came to an end and Stan was posted back to Waddington, a Vulcan bomber station. I got a job near the castle in Lincoln and we rented a ground floor flat in the St Catherine's area. The River Witham was at the bottom of the garden, however Stan found the 'coarse' fishing there rather tame, after the variety of tropical fish in Labuan! Eventually we were granted a married quarter 'on camp' at Waddington and it was then that I settled into life as an 'RAF wife'. I made friends with other wives and joined the archery club and a singing group.

Waddington was a very busy station in the front line of the 'Cold War'. Every day there was the sound of the huge aircraft engines being tested and aircraft taking off and landing. When four Vulcans 'scrambled', it was an impressive sight. The noise was tremendous and the ground shook as they took off one after another. Dispersal exercises were a regular part of life, usually beginning in the middle of the night. Land Rovers would tour the site, sirens blaring, bells ringing and horns tooting. Airmen would get up and rush to their jobs on site, to get aircraft ready to disperse to airfields all over the country. Wives were left hoping it was just a 'practice' - the thought of it being the 'real thing' was too awful to contemplate. Stan would usually go off to a dispersal airfield and return days later, tired and hungry. Once he had been to Macrihanish in Scotland and brought home some shellfish!

Our two sons were born during our time at Waddington. They grew up totally used to the sound of aircraft noise and were rarely woken by the sirens of the Alerts. I recall one time when Adam was a few weeks old: he was asleep in his pram in the garden and Alex was playing nearby. A Vulcan roared over the house, much lower than I had ever seen one and I feared it was going to crash. Alex continued playing and Adam slept on. The aircraft did not crash!

Winters in Lincolnshire were extremely cold, with snow and freezing fog. Wives had to endure very cold husbands coming home in the middle of the night and creeping into bed to get warm. Sometimes there were problems with the married quarters. One year there was a heavy snowfall during the night, followed by a very fast thaw the following day. As the snow melted, it penetrated the poorly-insulated roof and when I went upstairs and opened a wardrobe door, I was met by a rush of water. Water was also dripping through the ceilings of the bedrooms in various places. At the time I was 6 months' pregnant. When Stan came home, he went into the loft, filled buckets with water and passed them down to me to empty. Over 40 houses had been affected and the following summer all had to have their roofs removed and properly insulated.

Stan left the RAF in 1972 and we settled down to civilian life – never again to be awoken by sirens in the middle of the night!

Chapter 21: Mickey Finn Exercises

Previously, I have touched on the strategy of dispersing the V-Force to multiple airfields throughout the country in the event of a dangerous and imminent increase in the threat posed to NATO by the USSR. Bomber Command needed to be certain that all elements involved in the execution of such dispersion and the corresponding ramifications could work together like a well oiled machine. For this reason, it periodically sprang a surprise dispersal exercise on the entire V-Force. This exercise had the code name Mickey Finn. Announcement of the exercise came by way of the Station public address system – the Tannoy – and usually early in the morning before the normal 8 to 5 working day began. The Tannoy system didn't extend to the Station Married Quarters, so RAF Police Land Rovers patrolled its streets, verbally broadcasting the news from loudspeakers preceded by a loud Klaxon noise and tooting of the vehicle's horn. Married personnel off-base were contacted by a well established routine that involved one person being contacted by phone from the Station; that person then contacting a small number of other living-out personnel, who in turn contacted their own group of people. In this way, all off-base personnel were notified to get to their place of work immediately.

No one would be permitted to leave the camp until the exercise was over, other than to be ferried to a dispersal airfield. It was therefore considered prudent for those likely to be dispersed to have their small pack ready and close to hand at all times. In the small pack would be some changes of underwear, socks and maybe a clean shirt together with a set of toiletry items.

The object of the exercise was to generate as many aircraft as possible onto a war footing. That meant getting every aircraft that could be made serviceable ready to fly, which included those in the hangars undergoing second line servicing and probably devoid of much of their electrical and electronic equipment. Stores would be busy issuing serviceable components to replace the removed equipment. Of course, live weapons would not be loaded because it was government policy that V-bombers would never be airborne with nuclear weapons aboard unless the Cold War suddenly turned red hot. Instead, a nuclear weapon simulator was installed in the bomb bay. The simulator accepted all the inputs and provided all the feedback that a real weapon would, but of course could not be dropped. In appearance, it looked like a medium-sized box with some indicator lights on its surface. It was mounted in the bomb bay, where the appropriate connections could be plugged into it. In order to keep the Navigator Radar and Pilot honest, the simulator incorporated two detachable ferrite cores that were removed when the aircraft had landed and taken to the Armament Electrical Bay, where they were connected to an 'interrogator' device. The interrogator was able to demonstrate, by means of a matrix of lamps, whether or not the aircrew had operated the correct switches and set up the appropriate conditions for the particular exercise in which the sortie had been flown. It was then a case of 'jolly good show' or a 'bollocking', depending on the results obtained.

As part of the exercise, we also loaded four large dispensers of aluminium chaff, code named 'Window', into each aircraft, which could be dropped to confuse enemy radar. It was a backup to the more sophisticated Electronic Counter Measures (ECM) that the Vulcan B1A and B2 carried in its bulbous tail. The thin strips of chaff were contained in a series of small cardboard packets, called bundles. Each bundle measured approximately 10 inches by 2 inches and was glued onto two continuous, parallel strips of reinforced cardboard tape. The chaff was loaded into the dispensers like ammunition belts and the ends of the tapes fed into a machine that could be programmed by the AEO to drop a certain number of bundles at certain time intervals. When activated, cogs in the machine pulled the double tapes into openings. When a bundle arrived at the machine, it couldn't follow the tapes through the holes that led to the cogs, so the little cardboard package was ripped off and from there, fell out of the aircraft through a chute on the underside of each wing. The action of being ripped off the tapes also unsealed the packets, so that when they hit the slipstream, they opened up and spilled out the multiple strips of aluminium foil. A continuous sequence of bundles falling out of the Vulcan left a stream of chaff in its wake, which had the effect of appearing on enemy radar screens as a green cloud that hid the Vulcan. It was an old trick, first used in the Second World War, but still worked when all else failed.

One of an electrician's jobs was to functionally test the Window dispensing system. This was performed in a very sophisticated way. One electrician would sit in the AEO's position whilst his mate would go to one of the four chute exits. And now for the sophisticated part – he took off his beret and held it bowl-like just below the chute. The first electrician could see the second through the AEO's periscope and when his mate had assumed the correct position, he selected to drop one bundle from the Window control panel. If all went according to plan, the packet of chaff would drop into the upheld beret without spilling out its contents. As can be imagined, things sometimes didn't quite go according to plan when Murphy's Law reared its ugly head in a number of ways. The cable identification sleeves could be missing or indecipherable, resulting in cross-connected Window control panels at the AEO's station; it was possible for the man performing the drop to select the one particular dispenser when his mate was actually at the chute of another; periscopes were not installed in all Vulcans, which meant that good communication between the two was essential, although not always perfect. Airfield radar sometimes got knocked out for a lengthy period when something like this happened, although it was a very rare occurrence. But I digress, so will now get back to the subject of Mickey Finns.

When any given Vulcan had been recovered, i.e. was fully ready for simulated war, it was despatched to its assigned dispersal airfield. Meanwhile, ground crews would already have been sent ahead. Ground transport was employed for those airfields that were not too distant. One that I had personally been sent to was RAF Leconfield, near Beverly in Yorkshire and home, at that time, to one or more English Electric Lightning squadrons.

We set off in a convoy of lorries, Land Rovers, a bus and a lorry towing an enclosed trailer, similar to those used to transport gliders, but larger, which contained an inert nuclear weapon. On the way there, we passed through a small village and at an intersection, where we had slowed down, an elderly lady waved urgently at the driver of the vehicle that was towing the nuke trailer and pointed at the trailer's wheel, which had smoke pouring out of the centre. It appeared to be an overheated bearing. The driver pulled over to take care of the problem, but I couldn't help wondering what the woman would have thought, had she known what the trailer was carrying.

At RAF Leconfield, we were a self-contained unit on an exclusively dedicated ORP near the northern end of the runway. Caravans, identical to those on the QRA dispersal were in place to house us and there was a field kitchen to provide meals. Being at the end of the runway, we had front row view of the Lightnings as they came in to land. Their approach speed seemed incredibly fast and the small, skinny wheels were so close together that it made me wonder how the pilots could accomplish the landings safely.

Eventually, our Vulcans arrived and we got involved in the process of seeing them in, carrying out post flight inspections and refuelling them. Unlike QRA, we had some leisure time and since the quaint town of Beverly was nearby, many of us made our way there for an evening out in the local pubs. Then, after two days at Leconfield, the order came for the Vulcans to go to 5 minute readiness and eventually to scramble and fulfil the remaining part of the Mickey Finn exercise before returning to Waddington. For the groundcrew, it meant packing up the dispersal area and then climbing aboard the bus for the ride home.

On another occasion, I was sent on a Mickey Finn exercise to RAF Kinloss, in northern Scotland, not far from Loch Ness. Kinloss was too distant from Waddington to get there by bus trip, so the groundcrew detailed for that dispersal station flew up there in a Transport Command Hercules. It was my first time in a 'Herky Bird' and I can only say that it was the most uncomfortable plane trip I've ever taken. The seats were mere webbing slings arrayed along the side of the fuselage on either side of the cargo space. There were no portholes so the interior of the cavernous cargo space was illuminated by dim lighting. The heating system, such as it was, alternately roasted us and then chilled us. Hot when the heated air was blasted into the interior and then chilly when it went off. This cycle played out over and over as the flight progressed. Several of us asked the Air Quarter Master if we could visit the flight deck. When it was my turn, I clambered up the few steps to stand behind the pilots. It was much nicer up there with bright light from the cockpit windows. The pilots, wearing American style baseball caps (headgear that our Vulcan pilots wouldn't have been caught dead wearing while in flight) were friendly and inviting.

Eventually, we landed at Kinloss and assumed our Mickey Finn duties. I was struck by the clarity of the air there. It had the feel of the atmospheric conditions at my home in Northern Ireland, although 'home' was a long way south of there.

We spent the usual couple of days at Kinloss, but there was no nearby town to visit and we were somehow isolated out on the airfield with no way to get to anywhere anyway, so we spent all of our stay there at the dispersal area. At the end of the exercise, the Vulcans scrambled and then we waited for the Hercules to come and ferry us home. And we waited and waited before eventually receiving the news that our Hercules had become unserviceable and that there would be a long delay before it could make the trip up to Kinloss to pick us up. After a long, several hours wait, the Herky Bird finally showed up. We boarded with our equipment, took off, did one circuit of the airfield and then landed again. It had gone unserviceable again! Another long wait before we were allowed to board again. This time, when we took off, we headed home to Waddington for a very late arrival.

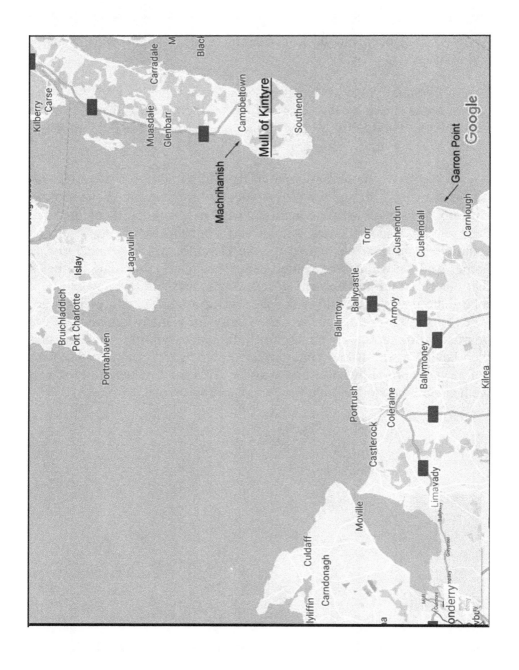

Chapter 22: The Machrihanish Incident

Another of Waddington's dispersal airfields was located on the western side of the Mull of Kintyre, which is a substantial peninsula that dives south from the Scottish mainland and almost collides with the coast of Northern Ireland. I know this well, because I attended a grammar school on Garron Point in County Antrim for a year and on a clear day, could clearly see the end of the Mull across the Irish Sea, which was just a little over 18 miles away.

The dispersal airfield on the Mull is named Machrihanish (Mack-rah-hannish), which nowadays serves as Campbeltown Airport. When viewed on Google Earth, one can see the individual V-bomber dispersal pans that still remain on the north side of the main runway. They are eight in number and appear as circular areas of asphalt connected by a taxiway to either a main taxiway or, in two cases, directly to the main runway.

I never had the pleasure of visiting this particular dispersal airfield, but am aware of an incident that occurred when a Mickey Finn dispersal exercise dispatched a flight of four Vulcans and supporting ground crew to that remote location. Geoff Supple, my friend and fellow electrician on Line Squadron, remembers it well. Probably that's because he was one of the main instigators of the incident, together with Barry Goodall. Here is the story of the incident mostly in Geoff's own words, which he wrote some 50 years after the event. His words are in italics with my occasional inserts in normal type.

It's 50 years ago that Britain was at the height of the COLD WAR. The weekend and days leading up to the 27th/28th October 1962 saw the World on the brink of a Nuclear War during the Cuba Missile Crisis.

Subsequent years had Britain and the V-Bomber Force at a high state of readiness. Vulcans were often deployed to Dispersal Airfields on exercise during these times. RAF Machrihanish in Argyllshire was one such airfield.

RAF Machrihanish 1963 possibly 1964

I was a 19 year old aircraft technician working on the Vulcan Bomber. A small detachment of Vulcans and their ground crew had flown to RAF Machrihanish as part of a major exercise.

On completion of the 2-day exercise, the Vulcans were scrambled and flew back to base in Lincolnshire. This left the remaining ground crew waiting for a transport aircraft to fly them back sometime in the afternoon.

We asked the Detachment Commander if we could go for a wander and he granted us permission, provided we were back in time to fly back to RAF Waddington in Lincolnshire. The aircraft was due to land mid-afternoon.

So, four or five of us walked along the dunes to the Golf Club. Although it was only mid-morning, they were very hospitable and opened up the bar for us!

Campbeltown

After having had a beer or two with the members, someone got us a taxi into Campeltown and we continued our Goodwill Tour. Sometime during the lunchtime revelry, we met up with a local lad who was probably the same age as us.

As we were hungry, he suggested that we go to his Aunt's café, where we could get a good fry-up for lunch.

During our chat with Jock (not very p.c., I know, but we never knew his name), he asked us if we were going to go to the local dance.

We obviously couldn't, but told him about the great dance nights that we had back at base. Similarly, on a Thursday.

Suddenly, an irate Detachment Commander appeared in the café and informed us that the Transport Command Argosy was landing earlier than expected and we were to get into the Land Rover and back to base.

In amongst all of the hubbub, I suggested to Jock that he come back with us to Lincolnshire and come to our dance on base.

Before long, Jock was kitted out with an anorak, a beret and a tool bag and was standing waiting for the Argosy to taxi in and pick us all up!

The giveaway was his shoes, which were Italian style with buckles as opposed to heavy boots which we all wore. Nobody in authority seemed to notice though!

At one stage, a sergeant asked him to marshal in the Argosy, which had landed. Fortunately, a friend of mine jumped up and said that he would do it.

Jock confessed that he had never been away from Scotland before, let alone fly in an aircraft.

The roll was called, but no headcount, so far, so good! Strapped in, rolling and then we were airborne………

RAF Waddington

An hour and a bit later, I was awakened by a nudge from the guy sat next to me to say that we were about to land. OMG! What was going on?? It all flooded back to me and I realized that this was going to take some explaining. I'd probably get locked up in The Tower until I was old enough to know better!

*Our luck was in, though. We had not been sussed yet. I asked Jock to do his seat belt up and, it transpired, that he hadn't **undone** it since our takeoff in Scotland! We were met at the aircraft by a coach, which took us all to the Airmen's Mess, where we indulged in a meal to rival (Jock's) Auntie's café grub.*

(Jock then) came back to our accommodation block and we soon found him a spare bed and bedding. The next stage of our adventure was about to get under way.

By now, (Jock) was a bit of a celebrity and by the time we arrived at The Wheatsheaf, which is a pub in the local (Waddington) *village, word seemed to have got around about the escapade. I remember one of the Aircrew, who was a regular in The Wheatsheaf, shaking his head in disbelief.*

The Thursday night dance was everything that we had promised him, with a great band and lots of local girls.

Next came the problem of getting him back to Scotland. He told me that if he could get to Glasgow by 3 pm, there was a bus down the Mull of Kintyre that would get him back to Campbeltown! A mere 416 miles to do in 1963......mmmnnnnnn, it may take more than the hour and a bit it took (for him) *to get to England!!*

The next morning, I woke our new-found friend early. No time for breakfast. I walked him up to the top (Lincoln to Grantham) *road, where I began thumbing a lift for him. The first car stopped and a rather bemused driver listened intently as I gave him strict instructions to drop Jock in Grantham, which was 25 miles away, point him NORTH on the A1 and Robert's your Mum's brother!!*

Although the Squadron Commander dropped various comments over the following days, nothing was ever said on an official basis. So maybe after 50 years, I've got away with it...............

Somewhere in Campbeltown, a guy exists who told this story to his girlfriend when he didn't show up for their date on Thursday evening. I'll bet he had some difficulty convincing her, his mum and everyone of his epic adventure........

The follow-up

At the time, on realizing what he had done while under the influence of a few beers, Geoff was only too pleased to get Jock back on the road to Scotland and by doing so, avoided the very real possibility of finding himself on the carpet and facing some serious disciplinary action. But years later, after having written his recollection of the incident and being an older and wiser man, he began wondering what actually happened to Jock. Did he make it back to Campbeltown? Did he go in the right direction on the A1? Did he perhaps find somewhere more interesting and preferable to the Mull of Kintyre, where he might have settled down instead of making his way home? With these questions floating around inside his head, Geoff decided to try to find out. So he sent a copy of the story you have just read to the *Campbeltown Courier*, which printed it along with a call for 'Jock' to contact them if he remembered his clandestine trip to the land of the Sassenachs.

Several months later, Geoff received a personal message from a Campbeltown resident, through social media, inviting contact by email. When Geoff emailed the man, his response spoke of a regular at his local pub who had described a personal experience that was strikingly similar to Geoff's tale in the *Courier*. Geoff's correspondent then provided a telephone number and suggested that he should call it; the obvious implication being that it was Jock's phone number. Unfortunately, no one ever answered on the several occasions that Geoff rang the number. Geoff's informant might have been dismissed as a hoaxer, except for one thing – he mentioned an escapade that the story teller in the pub had claimed to have participated in during his visit to Waddington. Geoff had completely forgotten about it and therefore had not included it in the story he sent to *The Courier*, but he remembered the incident when the man's mention of it jogged his memory. From this, we can surmise with some confidence that Jock did indeed find his way home and lived to tell the tale, probably earning a few free pints in the telling of his grand adventure. As for the escapade at Waddington – sorry, but Geoff prefers to apply a well known rule to that part of the tale – "What happened in the WRAF Block stays in the WRAF Block!"

Chapter 23: Exercise Sunspot

Some exercises were planned in advance, eliminating the surprise element. One of those was the annual Sunspot exercise that involved a 4-week detachment to RAF Luqa on the Mediterranean island of Malta, in May or June of each year. Luqa was shared with the Maltese Civil Aviation Authority, who used it as Malta's airport. One of the objectives of Sunspot was to engage the Vulcan aircrews in bombing practice using conventional iron bombs. The Vulcan was capable of carrying 21 x 1,000-pound bombs in its bomb bay, which the crews dropped on the RAF El Adem bombing range in the Libyan Desert, which was a 500 mile hop across the Mediterranean from Malta.

The May 1964 detachment included sufficient groundcrew members, of which I was fortunate to be one, that were considered necessary to support and maintain four Vulcans. Personally, it was my first ever overseas trip to a sunnier, warmer climate, so I was looking forward to it immensely. On the appointed day, we departed on an RAF Transport Command Bristol Britannia – a large four-engine turboprop, passenger aircraft nicknamed The Whispering Giant because of its relative quietness compared to jet aircraft and those propelled by piston engines. The seats were comfortable and the cabin conditioning maintained the air temperature at an agreeable level. Meals were not so comparable to those provided on civil airliners; we were handed a cold lunch by the Air Quartermaster, consisting of a salad together with some typical RAF airmen's mess curled up sandwiches and the inevitable hard-boiled egg 'airmen, for the consumption of'.

I can't recall how long the flight took, but based on the approximate distance of Malta from Waddington and the cruising speed of a Britannia, it was probably around 6 hours. However long the flight lasted, it was late afternoon when the coastline of Malta flashed below as we came in to land. We had enplaned at Waddington wearing standard RAF tropical uniforms with which we had been issued a few days prior to our departure. It was the ugly, unflattering KD (khaki drill) that most servicemen on tropical overseas postings soon dumped in favour of a locally tailored version. For brief detachments, however, such as Sunspot, we had no option but to wear the official KD. It

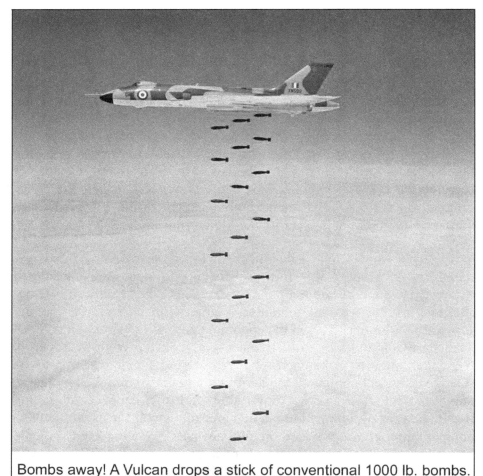

Bombs away! A Vulcan drops a stick of conventional 1000 lb. bombs.

consisted of knee length, baggy, KD shorts for daytime wear and KD trousers for night time, combined with long-sleeved 'Airtex' shirts. During daylight hours, the order of dress was to roll the sleeves up to above the elbow. After dark, when worn with trousers, the sleeves were to be rolled down and buttoned at the wrist. At least we didn't have to wear ties.

Darkness had fallen by the time we deplaned, so we couldn't see much of our surroundings, although I remember seeing a massive palm tree lit by a street lamp as we were marched to the barrack block in which we would be accommodated during the month-long duration of the exercise. Half of the men were stood down, most of whom

Bristol Brittania of Royal Air Force Transport Command

planned on heading into Valletta, the capital city, to sample its delights. Unfortunately, I was amongst the other half for whom it was a matter of dumping our kit on a chosen bed, changing into our KD trousers and rolling down our sleeves, before being transported across to the V-bomber dispersal area on the other side of the airfield so that we could welcome in our Vulcans, which were manned by one of the Waddington squadron aircrews, possibly 101 Squadron. Valletta would have to wait.

The next morning, those of us for whom this was our first detachment to Luqa were detailed to attend a briefing to familiarize us with the station and with Malta in general. I don't recall too much about what was said at the briefing, but it included reminders that we were in a foreign country and to behave ourselves in ways that wouldn't bring discredit to the RAF. The order of dress, which meant when to wear KD shorts with sleeves rolled up and when to wear the long trousers with sleeves rolled down and buttoned, was explained. There were also suggestions on what to see during our off duty hours and how to get around the island. We were invited to ask questions, one of which I particularly remember. An airman stood up and asked about the water and if it was 'brackish'. I had never heard that word before and didn't really know what it meant, but it didn't sound good. The officer giving the briefing didn't truly answer the question, but mentioned that the water on Malta did taste different from what we were used to back home. Later I discovered this for myself, because it had an unpleasant taste as did the tea in the airmen's mess. Some people claimed that the taste of the tea in the mess was due to the use of goat's milk instead of cow's milk, but I firmly believe it was due to the 'brackish' water.

The detachment did not involve a night shift, so the next evening I was free to explore the delights of Valletta with some of the other squadron lads. That night, my introduction to its nightlife was confined to Strait Street, better known to British military men as The Gut. It was a street of seamy bars populated by young boys who approached seemingly out of nowhere, addressing us by the generic name of 'John' and each wanting to know if we would like to meet his sister, exclaiming, "She virgin!"

"No thanks!"

Embarrassing as it is to admit now at my advanced age, the main objective of visiting The Gut, for those of us in my then age group, was to get drunk as quickly and as inexpensively as possible. This was easily accomplished by purchasing a bottle of Marsovin – a local white wine that had a taste akin to paint thinners, it was nicknamed Screech. A bottle of Screech cost the bargain price of 1/2d (one shilling and tuppence) and we were probably being ripped off at that price. To mask the taste, we also purchased a bottle of Coke and mixed it with the wine. The desired effect was accomplished very quickly and the remainder of the evening saw us to staggering around, vomiting, peeing, acting like idiots and generally making fools of ourselves. Great fun!

The Gut's large preponderance of bars included such exotic names as *The Egyptian Queen*, (or the *Gypo Queen* to those of us visiting it). Other favourites included *Carmen's* and *The Bing Crosby Bar*. Sitting in these establishments always invited company in the form of young women who, when not seated with a male customer, hung around the bar in small groups talking amongst themselves. When customers entered the bar and sat down, the barman would nod towards the new arrivals, while looking meaningfully at the girls. This was their

Two of the many bars in The Gut.

Photo: Jack Birns © Time Life, Inc.

cue to go and sit down at the table, each of them next to a customer. And let's be clear here; the customers were Royal Navy sailors or their equivalents from the U.S. fleet, or RAF types like us. Maltese men, other than the bar owners, wouldn't be caught dead in such scurvy places.

When seated beside a customer in a pouty pose, the girls would ask, in heavily accented English, "Hello Johnny, you buy me drink?"

Most often, those of us on Sunspot would ignore the girls and concentrate on the serious business of becoming inebriated, but when someone did buy one of the ladies a drink, it was nothing more than a tiny glass of peppermint liquid. At the same time, she would receive a token from the barman, which she would presumably cash in at the end of her shift for some small pittance.

I don't recall how we got to Valletta that evening or how we got back, but it was probably by taxi. On the weekends, we were able to go in to see the city in daylight and explore the main street, avoiding The Gut, which was exclusively reserved for rollicking night-time escapades.

Getting to Valletta or anywhere else on the island, while avoiding the costlier taxis, was by means of the local bus service; a service that bore little resemblance to the Lincolnshire Roadcar bus service to which we were accustomed back at Waddington. The only thing that the two services had in common was that both conveyed paying passengers, but any similarity ended abruptly there. The garishly painted and highly decorated Maltese buses had the appearance of being home-made, or having been put together in some back alley workshop. No two looked alike. The passenger seating consisted of hard, uncomfortable park bench-like seats that transmitted the jar of every bump in the road to the backside and spine of the passenger. Everything vibrated and rattled as the bus bounced along at seemingly breakneck speed over the uneven road surfaces. Tyres shrieked on the shiny tarmac at the slightest change in direction, which only added to the 'thrill' of the ride.

Malta is something of a tourist destination nowadays, so perhaps things have improved, but at that time the roads were little more than paved, bumpy, meandering tracks of irregular and narrow width, mostly bordered by low dry stone walls. Here and there, the conjoined, oval paddles of large prickly cactus plants reared up along the roadsides like set decorations in a Clint Eastwood spaghetti western. Traffic on the roads was chaotic and paid little attention to the Highway Code – if there actually was one. The buses careened along the these roads with the driver rarely braking but blaring the bus's very loud horn instead, narrowly missing other buses, cars, brave pedestrians and flocks of goats. The other vehicles, not to be outdone, used their horns and saved their brakes as enthusiastically as the bus drivers.

A niche at the front of the passenger compartment, in virtually all of the buses, housed a small religious shrine containing a statue of a saint or the Virgin Mary, usually surrounded by artificial flowers. Many more religious and pop culture decorations vied for space around the walls above curtained windows. This décor was generally true of every bus, although they were distinctly individual in the actual selection of decorations. But the strangest thing of all was that the steering wheel was located in the centre of the driving position, while the driver's seat was offset to the right hand side. This resulted in the driver having to reach over to his left to steer the bus. The reason for this it was said, (although I'm not sure it was true), was that St. Christopher actually drove the bus and the driver was only there to assist him. So, dear old St. Chris had the wheel, although we mere mortals were unable actually see him. It was also said that if and when a situation became too dodgy, the driver simply let go of the wheel, closed his eyes and left all of the driving up to St. Christopher. Thankfully, that particular scenario never occurred during any of my trips, so I never actually discovered how well the saint could handle the bus without the driver's assistance.

Weekends gave us more time to sample some of the other pleasures of the island, especially during daylight hours that allowed us to enjoy the sunny climate. Much of the activity involved going on swimming expeditions in the warm Mediterranean Sea, at various places around the coast. Sometimes we would take a taxi to a picturesque bay known as Marsaxlokk where small, colourful Maltese rowing boats bobbed in the waves or were pulled up on the beach around the bay, each brightly painted and decorated in reds and yellows and greens. But we weren't there to see the boats; we had come to swim in the nearby Peter's Pool. One of the other places that could be reached by riding in the infamous Maltese buses was Golden Bay. At other times, we went to another location known as the Blue Grotto. This was the life!

One weekend, an American aircraft carrier, the USS Forrestal, paid a courtesy visit to Malta. It was part of the U.S. Navy's 6th Fleet that patrols the Mediterranean. The ship's crew had shore leave; consequently, white U.S. naval uniforms were everywhere. Some of our lads met up with a group of officers from the carrier and were invited to go aboard, which they did. They were treated courteously and one later showed me a souvenir Zippo cigarette lighter on which the ship's name was engraved, which he had been given as a souvenir.

One of the interesting things about Malta was that most of the buildings were constructed of sandstone. It possessed some splendid architecture, not least of which were its many churches surmounted by magnificent domes. There was also a large, ornate fountain on the approach to Valletta, known as the Triton Fountain. Geoff Supple surmises that somewhere in Malta there is an elderly retired Police Officer who probably recalls persuading him and Barry Goodall to get out of the Fountain and return to base, before he called for reinforcements!

The same pair of 'eejits' in the company of two others, Mick Spiring and 'Ginge' Jones, decided to avail themselves of the services of a horse drawn carriage, known in Malta as a Karrozin, (but nicknamed a Gharry by the British military, in memory of a similar mode of transport of that name in India, during the days of the British Raj). Prior to taking the ride, the four erks had spent considerable time in The Gut and were well and truly feeling its effects. They had each also decided to bring some of The Gut with them in the form of bottles of Screech. After polishing off the contents of the bottles, they then began imagining that the Gharry was a Wild West stagecoach and that the innocent Maltese pedestrians were marauding redskins. Using the empty bottles to mimic six-guns, they pretended to shoot the unsuspecting passers-by to the accompaniment of vocal 'shooting' sounds and loud laughter. History does not record what the Gharry driver thought, but as long as he got his money, it's a fair bet he thought he was just pleased to be rid of those crazy Englishmen.

However, 'eejits' don't need to be full of Screech to do stupid stuff. Boredom sometimes works just as well. On one particular day we had to be on shift for a full 24 hours in the furtherance of some kind of exercise. Most of the 24 hours was spent sitting around, sometimes nodding off for forty winks, but soon to be awakened because it wasn't allowed. Sitting in a shed that served as the Electrical Section, we were bothered by pesky flies that were more aggressive than their better mannered British counterparts, as well as being more numerous and infinitely more agile. Attempting to swat them was ineffective because they seemed to possess a heightened awareness of impending attacks and usually escaped long before the swatter connected with where they had just been. Around that time, our stores had acquired a type of lubricating grease that was applied in an aerosol spray from a can. The grease was dissolved in the propellant, but soon solidified when the latter evaporated. It turned out to be the perfect weapon against the quick-witted flies. A passing, in-flight, insect was a much better target than one that sat ready to leap into the air at the slightest hint of being swatted. The broad, diverging cone of spray from the aerosol could easily be aimed to envelope the fly with only a casual effort at accuracy. Once sprayed, the fly flew on – but only for a short distance, just long enough for the propellant to evaporate. When the grease solidified, the hapless creature dropped to the ground like a stone, where it could be summarily dealt with. I hope the British taxpayers never find out what we did with the grease that their hard earned, confiscated tax money paid for.

***

Part of the Sunspot exercise included an Air Defence Exercise in which our Vulcans played the role of the bad guys, with Malta being defended by RAF fighters. At the conclusion of the exercise, all four aircraft were scheduled to return to Luqa, but as luck would have it, the third of the detachment's four Vulcans burst all of its tyres on the starboard undercarriage when landing. I have a memory of seeing the hapless Vulcan taxiing a short distance along the runway with fragments of tyre flapping from its main wheels. It didn't roll far in that condition and came to a halt, effectively blocking the main runway. Riggers were then dispatched out there with a set of replacement wheels and all the necessary tools and equipment to perform a complete wheel change on that side. Meanwhile, the fourth Vulcan was still airborne, but obviously couldn't land at Luqa, so it was diverted to the Royal Navy Fleet Air Arm airfield at RNAS Hal Far, on the south edge of the island.

Next morning, back out at the dispersal bright and early, a few of us were detailed as a starter crew for the Vulcan stranded at Hal Far. Only a few of our number were assigned to drive the RAF vehicles at our disposal, but I didn't mind one little bit to have someone else dicing with the Maltese traffic; being a passenger was nerve-wracking enough. There were about four of us, so we got in a Land Rover, driven by one of the lads, and set off for Hal Far, arriving there around the same time that most of the navy people were showing up for their day of mateloting, or splicing the mainbrace, or whatever navy people did.

The Vulcan was parked just inside the main gate, close to the end of the runway. The Crew Chief had probably been there the previous night, after the aircraft had landed, because proper Vulcan chocks were in place. More than likely, there had been an RAF Police guard on duty overnight, given the level of security surrounding V-bombers during that period and the proximity of the Vulcan to the Hal Far boundary fence and outside road.

The arriving naval personnel were visibly startled by the huge delta-winged beast that had descended on their airfield in the middle of the night; more so because it was parked conspicuously near where they entered the base. Obviously, work for Hal Far was going to be a little late getting started that day because a crowd had gathered to watch as we strange RAF types (in our ugly KD) got to work on recovering the Vulcan and getting it airborne. It must have seemed strange to them that it took so many of us to accomplish the task; however, we went about our job like the, *ahem*, professionals we were.

Farewell Hal Far

Photo courtesy of Eric Bickley-Faux from his father Barry Bickley's collection

There was no 112 volt DC power available at Hal Far, which the engine starter motors needed, but that wasn't a problem. The Vulcan used its on-board batteries. The 24 volt DC battery powered the cockpit instruments and control circuits, while the number 1 engine could be started from the 96 volt DC battery. Number 1 was started and when it was up to speed and its 112 volt DC generator on line, the pilot used its power to start the three other engines. Soon, all engines were running and then it was 'chocks away' when directed by the Crew Chief, with just some marshalling to point the Vulcan towards the runway threshold, only a few yards distant. Our show-off pilot then treated the assembled matelots to a spectacularly noisy take off run along the length of the runway before rotating the Vulcan and soaring up at 45° angle, high into the morning sky, leaving a trail of black smoke and ear-splitting crackling noise in its wake. We all felt immensely proud, certain that our sailor brethren were suitably awed and impressed, as we gathered up the chocks and headed back to Luqa.

Too soon, our time in the sun was drawing to an end. Arrangements were being made for our return to a more mundane life at Waddington. Although we had been ferried out to Luqa in the relative comfort of a Royal Air Force Transport Command's Bristol Britannia, our return journey was not to be as auspicious. We learned that four Handley Page Hastings had been assigned to fly out from RAF Lyneham to pick us up. Unlike the turboprop powered Britannia, the Hastings was propelled at a slower speed by four piston engines. It was also unpressurized and the seating consisted of backwards facing steel seats covered by a very thin cushion.

Passenger lists were circulated and my name appeared on that of the second aircraft scheduled to arrive. The first Hastings arrived on time and those assigned to it boarded and were soon on their way. We of the second load waited expectantly for our aircraft to make its scheduled appearance, but close to the time at which it should have been there, we were informed that it had been delayed at Lyneham due to an engine oil leak. Subsequently, the third Hastings arrived, those on its passenger list boarded and they too were soon on their way. Still no second Hastings by the time the fourth arrived. It too took its passengers on board and took off into the wide blue yonder. We of the second batch were left frustrated, wondering if we were ever going to get out of there. To make matters worse, Al Hewitt had received a letter from his girlfriend in which she told him of a dream she had had in which the aircraft he would be on was going to crash on the way home.

Thank you very much! She shouldn't have put that in her letter and Al should definitely have kept it to himself. Because he shared her comment, many of us felt a bit spooked. I know that I certainly did no doubt because I was still having problems as a result of the car crash he and I had been in not too many months previously. Now, here we were, waiting for a long overdue Hastings that had been delayed because of an oil leak and we were being told of a premonition that it might crash. Not a good start to the trip home!

Finally, our aircraft arrived. Refuelling commenced, carried out by Maltese 'local' RAF personnel. These men were literally recruited locally and were paid at a rate consistent with the Maltese economy. So, although they wore RAF uniforms, their RAF service was strictly confined to the island of Malta.

When given the go-ahead, we boarded the Hastings. The engines started and we settled in for the long trip home. The pilot ran each engine up, one by one, to full rpm and then checked the 'mag drop'. Each engine was equipped with two magnetos that produced the high voltage needed for the ignition plugs. For this routine piston engine test, one of the two magnetos is switched off and the drop in engine rpm noted. If the speed falls by more than a certain rpm, the 'mag drop' is deemed unacceptable. This test is then repeated with the other magneto. An unacceptable mag drop due to switching off either magneto meant that, at best, the ignition plugs (the 'spark' plugs) needed to be changed. At the worst, it meant that there could be a more serious problem with the ignition system. In our case, the mag drop on at least one of the engines was unacceptable. Things were going from bad to worse.

We deplaned so that the locals could change the plugs on the failed engine. Then, after another interminable wait, the re-plugged engine was started up and the mag drop checked again. It was promptly shut down. The mag drop was fixed, but now there was an oil leak. We were all beginning to feel uneasy by now; the girlfriend's dream, the oil leak at Lyneham, the mag drop and now a second oil leak that the Maltese locals were going to fix. Our confidence in their ability, I'm ashamed to say, wasn't very high, nor was our confidence in the engines that had so far exhibited so many problems, hence our heightened feelings of unease.

Eventually, we were allowed back on board the Hastings. I would have preferred that it was some other aircraft instead of this particular one, but there was no alternative. The engines were started, mag drop checks performed and this time they remained running. We taxied out to the runway and took off. So far, so good – no crash on take-off.

I was one of the last aboard and ended up at the rear end of the aircraft. It was just two or three rows up from what passed for a toilet on a Hastings – a small cubicle containing a chemical 'thunder box' that smelled to high heaven. Worse still, one of the lads near me was suffering from some gastric tract problems due to his having spent the previous night saying a fond, alcohol-fuelled farewell to The Gut. His frequent discharge of foul smelling intestinal gas permeated the whole rear end of the plane. To add to the problem, his affliction was aided by the aircraft's lack of pressurization, which meant that the surrounding air pressure was lower than at ground level because of our altitude. This aided the intensity and frequency of gas expulsions as his abdomen struggled to equalize its pressure with the outside atmosphere. Although those of us around the culprit complained long and loud, he just grinned back at us and kept on farting silent killers.

As the Hastings droned on, speech almost impossible over the noise of four piston engines and suffocation threatened from the putrid air in our vicinity, I pondered to myself – if we were fated by some anonymous girl's premonition to make an unscheduled, uncontrolled landing, where would it happen? Hopefully, not in some foreign land where it would not be easy to recover what was left of us. This became less of an academic and more of a realistic question when, somewhere over France, the Air Quarter Master informed us that the aircraft's radio antenna had become detached and was now something of a hazard. The antenna was the old fashioned type, essentially a long wire stretched between the cockpit roof and the top of the tailfin, like an airborne clothesline. According to the AQM, it had come loose from the cockpit end and was now wrapped around the tail. The bad omens just kept on piling up on top of each other!

After many hours had elapsed, we crossed The Channel and now I began thinking that if we came down, at least it would be on home ground and they could pick up our remains with less trouble. The Hastings flew on regardless. It got dark long before we started the descent and approach to Waddington. "Oh no!" I thought, "We've made it this far, just to crash on landing!" The main wheels touched the runway and we were nearly down. Okay, so maybe we're going to have a brake failure and crash off the end of the runway. At least that might be survivable. The tail wheel settled onto the tarmac, the Hastings slowed down and then turned off the runway and came to a stop at the Station Flight. We had made it! No big deal! Who was scared? Hey, not me.

Seriously, I have always loved flying and have never been afraid of the experience, neither before nor since that particular flight, but just that once...

Most of us had ordered and paid for duty-free stuff, so next day we had to go to the control tower to collect it from the H.M. Customs man because it had been brought back to Waddington 'in bond'. I had purchased a bottle of Haig's Dimple whiskey as a present for my soon-to-be father-in-law. Did I mention that Pam and I had got engaged in August 1963? I had also bought a carton of Benson & Hedges cigarettes for myself – and they were the English made version, not the foul tasting Maltese manufactured cigarettes. That reminds me to mention that although I enjoyed our fun-in-the-sun detachment to Malta, there were two things that I and many others disliked. One was the cigarettes that were sold on the island. I was a smoker at that time of my life and *Senior Service* was the brand that I regularly used. All of the British brands of cigarettes were readily available on Malta, including *Senior Service*, and they were less expensive than the same brands back home. The catch was that they were manufactured in Malta and the tobacco they contained was not the same variety as those made in England, consequently the smoke had a different, unpleasant taste. My other gripe is that the airman's mess tea had a very unpleasant taste because of the 'brackish' water that I mentioned earlier.

***

Shortly after my return from Exercise Sunspot, Pam and I got married on June 27th, 1964, in the picturesque St. Peter-in-Eastgate church that sits a stone's throw from the impressive Lincoln Cathedral. Because Stan was in Borneo, neither he nor Dorothy could be there, although we would have liked them to be. However, my side of the aisle was supported by Geoff Supple, 'Spike' Campion, Johnny Thorne and Carol, Artie Milne and Pauline, and 'Butch' Butcher and Connie. Pam and I were, in turn, invited as guests to the Thorne and Milne weddings as they occurred later in the year. Johnny Thorne followed Stan Eilbeck to Borneo soon afterwards because he too got posted there on a one-year unaccompanied tour.

'Spike' Campion (left) and author Brian Carlin being "photo-bombed" by the U.S. Navy while relaxing at the Triton fountain, Valletta.

Synchronized leap at Peter's Pool. Wally Ogilvie, Geoff Supple, Pete Knott, Barry Goodal.

Author Brian Carlin off-duty near his barrack block at Luqa.

Geoff Supple posed for this photo to impress fiancee Joan.

Chapter 24: The ORP Scrambles

The concrete apron adjoining the north (21) end of Waddington's runway was known as the ORP, an abbreviation for Operational Readiness Platform, from which nuclear armed Vulcans could have been scrambled in as little as 2 minutes in the event that the Cold War became white hot. For most of the Cold War, however, it was more often a demonstration stage, typically used during the annual Waddington 'Open Day' when the 2 minute scramble would be demonstrated to the awestruck spectators, or at other times to impress visiting dignitaries.

For the September 1964 Open Day, I was pleased to be detailed as a member of the groundcrew for the demonstration. There was an excitement to the event that was fun to be part of, but first there needed to be rehearsal. Four Vulcans were duly lined up on the angled dispersals from which they could roll right out onto the runway and, with a minimum of ground steering, be able to line up with the centreline while simultaneously accelerating at maximum takeoff thrust for the supposed one way trip to Russia. Flight Line Squadron's Junior Engineering Officer (JENGO), a pint-sized, baby-faced Flying Officer, was in charge of the groundcrew contingent. He organized the four crews so that each of us knew our role. One man was assigned to each wheel chock, one to the two ground power cables and one each to the two sets of Simstart cables; a total of five men per crew, plus the Crew Chief who was in charge of the Simstart trolley and in contact with the crew via the earphones in his aircrew helmet and his 'long lead'.

During our pre-rehearsal briefing, the JENGO lectured us on how we were to act, supposedly in a way that would reflect well on the RAF. Specifically, he emphasized that when we had performed our starter crew duties and the aircraft was taxiing out onto the runway, we were to sprint smartly to the side of the dispersal and line up, standing at attention. Clearly, he had no idea of the effect of a Vulcan's jet efflux as the aircraft blasted out of the dispersal with near wide open throttles. Anything or anyone not tied firmly down or sheltered from its immediate backwash would rapidly and unintentionally end up a fair distance from the dispersal. Mitch Mitchell, who served as a corporal

Vulcans on the ORP at Waddington, ready to scramble.

with me on Line Squadron, remembers on one ORP scramble that the protective steel panels on the petrol/electric ground power unit were torn off by jet blast and hurled far across the airfield. But getting back to our officer's ridiculous order, no one said anything, although we were all blessed with a strong instinct of self preservation.

With everyone in their place, including the aircrew, the signal was given for the rehearsal to begin. The Crew Chiefs of all four aircraft punched the buttons on their Simstart trolleys. Sixteen jet engines whined in unison as they wound up through their start sequences for the short time that it took them to reach idling speed. At the Crew Chiefs' signals, the Simstart cables and chocks were dragged away from each aircraft. Seconds later, when notified by their respective AEO, the Crew Chiefs indicated for the ground power cables to be removed. No sooner had that happened than the first aircraft lurched forward with its jet exhaust blasting out at full power. The strong jet efflux washed over the ORP, mixed with the loose soil and gravel that it picked up from the surrounding area, before the Vulcan swung around to line up with the runway. There was no way in hell that the starter crew could sprint smartly to the edge of the dispersal and stand to attention in an orderly line as the JENGO had ordered. They were too busy trying to find shelter behind ground equipment or whatever else in the vicinity provided cover – and there wasn't much of that. I remember diving to get behind a yellow runway marker while being peppered by dust and small pieces of gravel.

Afterwards, the diminutive officer threw a tantrum because we hadn't done what he had demanded. Someone tried to explain, but his words fell on deaf ears. The JENGO just insisted that we follow his order and line up after the scramble the next time, which would be the real thing on Open Day. I don't know why he put so much importance on this little pantomime act. After all, who amongst the spectators would be watching remote figures like us, even if we were dressed in white overalls? All attention would be on the four Vulcans thundering out of the ORP and into the sky.

That Saturday, it was 'show time'. Now outfitted in freshly laundered white overalls, we were positioned at the ORP, but instructed to stay out of sight in a caravan as we waited for our star turn. The aircrew were in an adjacent caravan. The scramble was one of the highlights of the Open Day displays and would come towards the end of the programme. I had been a spectator other years, while stationed at Cranwell, so had seen it all from that viewpoint. One thing I knew for sure was that no one in the spectator area, far away on the other side of the runway, was watching the ground crew to see if they all got in line after the scramble – all attention was focused on the scrambling Vulcans.

As our time to perform approached, the flying displays ceased and an expectant lull fell over the airfield. Although we couldn't hear it from our location, I knew that the commentator would be telling the crowd to direct their attention to the four Vulcans sitting across from them on the far side of the runway. He would tell them that we would initially go to a 5-minute state of readiness before getting the signal to scramble, at which time the Vulcans would become airborne in less than 2 minutes. This was our cue to sprint out of hiding and run towards the aircraft. All four Crew Chiefs opened the entrance doors in readiness for the aircrew to climb aboard, while the rest of us took up our assigned positions. For me, that was the starboard Simstart cables. My job would be to yank both cables out when signalled to do so by the Crew Chief. A few moments later, the aircrew arrived and emplaned. The Crew Chief closed the entrance door behind them. They began starting up the necessary systems, especially the PFCs – the Powered Flying Controls – because there wouldn't be time to start them all when we went to 2 minutes readiness; each control surface had its own PFC, something like ten PFCs in all.

Now we waited, presumably to create an air of suspense for the expectant onlookers; the announcer inviting them to check their wristwatches and time how long it took for all four Vulcans to become airborne from the initiation of the scramble. Then, when it was judged that sufficient time had passed to ramp up to the required level of drama, a green flare, fired from a Very pistol, arced through the air from the Airshow director's area in front of the crowd. The flare was mere theatrics because the real 'scramble' command came over the aircraft radio from the control tower and was simultaneously heard by all four aircrews and the Crew Chiefs. But the Very flare was a nice touch that let the spectators know that blue touch paper had been lit. Time for them to start the countdown!

On hearing the command over their headsets, the Crew Chiefs quickly pressed all four engine start buttons on the Simstart cart consoles in rapid succession. Immediately, the sound of the engines winding up could be heard and moments later, black exhaust smoke streamed out from the jet pipes of each Vulcan. My attention was focused on our Crew Chief, as was that of all the other members of the starter crew. When the engines reached self-sustaining speed, he raised both arms above his head and then rapidly pulled them down to his side, signalling for us to pull out the starter cables. Standing up on a main undercarriage wheel, I pulled on both of mine and then jumped down with the cables still in my grasp. The task now was to get them safely out of the way over at the edge of the dispersal. Next, the Crew Chief gave the 'chocks away' signal and both airmen assigned to that task dragged on the ropes attached to the heavy wooden chocks and got them out of the way too. Only the ground power cable remained plugged in. One solitary airman stood by it, waiting for the AEO to confirm that his generators were on line. On getting that 'okay', the Crew Chief then motioned for the power cable to be pulled out. The waiting airman yanked on it and then dragged it off to the side. Not wishing to be tumbled apex over teakettle across the airfield by the jet blast, he then dashed for cover behind the ground power unit. Next, the Crew Chief said his goodbyes to the on-board crew before unplugging his headset. He too then sprinted to find some shelter behind the GPU.

I don't recall to which of the four Vulcans I was assigned, but it certainly wasn't number one, which had already left the ORP. Straightening up on the runway, the pilot opened the four Olympus engines up to take-off power, sending the Vulcan roaring down the runway, leaving a cloud of black smoke in its wake. Lifting off, it clawed its way up into the sky, gaining altitude. About 10 seconds later, the second aircraft rolled onto the runway and repeated the first's performance, except that, where the first Vulcan had climbed to gain altitude, the second stayed on a lower, flatter take-off configuration to avoid the possibility of a collision. Meanwhile, clouds of dust, pebbles, and assorted detritus blasted across the ORP, from which we all did our best to take cover. As soon as it died away, I was able to look up in time to see the four Vulcans strung out in a smoky, noisy line. The two lead aircraft were already in the air, number three was just on the verge of rotating to leap into the air, while number four was still accelerating down the runway. In much less than two minutes from the firing of the Very flare, all four were airborne, easily demonstrating that the combined skills of aircrew and groundcrew were capable of fulfilling the RAF's readiness commitment. Afterwards, our JENGCO was strangely silent, nor did any of us ever hear or know of any fallout from disobeying his order.

Vulcans scrambling from the ORP. Only three are visible in the picture, because the fourth is obscured.

Photo courtesy of Eric Bickley-Faux from his father Barry Bickley's collection

The next day, minus our white overalls and our 15 minutes in the limelight behind us, those of us on the starter crews joined most of the other erks on the station, picking up litter and oh-so-nasty stuff that our visitors had kindly left behind as mementoes of their visit.

***

And now, the ORP experience through another pair of eyes. Geoff Supple recounts an experience that was originally published on the 'Vulcan to the Sky' website.

All this talk of QRAs, ORPs and the Cold War has brought back distant memories of my time as a young airman at RAF Waddington.

When the ORP was constructed, the Station Commander was very keen to demonstrate the Vulcan's capability as the UK's Airborne Nuclear Deterrent. There were several demonstrations where local dignitaries, NATO Military Staff and I guess anyone else who was on his Christmas card list were invited to witness this awesome spectacle.

Being on the Line Squadron in the early sixties, I had experience of our Cold War role and had been on QRA duties numerous times. We used the Sim Start Power to Rapid Start the engines but always ensured that the Main Power lead was not disconnected until the last possible moment. An insurance in case of Sim Start malfunction.

On one of these demonstrations, I was detailed for Starter Crew and given the task of final disconnection of the Main Power lead. The Crew Chief explained the drill, we were second in the order, and he seemed a bit nervous of the situation perhaps because of the spectator contingent just the other side of the runway.

"When the engines have started, the lads will disconnect the Sim Start leads and clear to the side of the dispersal." Pointing at me "Whatever you do, don't unplug the Power lead until I give you the signal"

So far so good..........

All going according to plan, engines start OK, Sim Start leads removed, crew clear to side of the dispersal. Crew Chief hesitates, no doubt watching the first aircraft move off.

Then he suddenly disconnected his headset and did a runner for the side of the dispersal. No signal, no message, not even a bleeding post card! In the best tradition of that other service, it was definitely a case of pull up the gangplank I'm alright jack!!

The fuselage moved and the engine noise got perceptibly louder. I removed the Power lead (two six as we used to say!) and not wishing to become the New Holder of the Lincolnshire Long Distance Somersaulting record decided to exit stage left. N.B. The record would probably never have been ratified due to the Jet pipe exhaust assistance, but I had no intention of putting it to the test!

I moved swiftly towards the rear of the Port Main undercarriage and continued at an Olympic pace to the side of the pan. It's said that at times like that your whole life passes before you... I was only a young airman and perhaps, unless you count that night behind the NAAFI the previous week there wasn't a lot of life to flash past...........

I digress.

Reaching the side of the pan one of the Sim Start lads asked the Crew Chief what had happened to the signal. "Oh, sorry about that." said he. "C'mon, I'll get you all a cup of tea!"

All's well that ends well. The massed spectators were none the wiser and oblivious to the fact that they had nearly witnessed someone rolling all the way to Washingborough!!!!

Geoff Supple RAF Waddington 1962-68

Chapter 25: All Postings Lead to Scampton

On that September day on the ORP, I had been stationed at Waddington for all of a year and a half, give or take a few days. Little did I know that my time at this, my favourite station of my entire RAF service, was coming to an end. One month later in mid-October, as I alighted from the day shift bus on arriving at The Line, Sergeant Renshaw, the squadron Admin NCO, took Butch Butcher and me aside and indicated that we follow him to his desk in the squadron's open office area. There, he informed us that we had both been posted to RAF West Raynham and that we were to report to the Station Orderly Room at Station Headquarters without delay.

On our way there in a squadron Land Rover, Butch confided that he and his wife Connie had recently purchased a brand new house in Lincoln and that he did not want to be posted. He said that he was going to try to get out of it some way.

When we presented ourselves at SHQ, it transpired that we had been selected to become members of a very special, newly formed, multi-national squadron whose task it was to evaluate how the revolutionary Hawker Siddeley P1127 vertical takeoff aircraft could be best employed in a military environment. We would be working jointly with members of the American and German armed services in the unique Kestrel Evaluation Squadron; 'Kestrel' was the name given to the nine aircraft ordered by the Ministry of Defence for this purpose. Although disappointed at having to leave Waddington, where I had made many firm friends, I was equally excited at the prospect of joining such a unique and potentially historic squadron. Butch, on the other hand, was totally unfazed by the special nature of our posting. He obviously couldn't use the purchase of his new house as a reason to have his posting cancelled, but within a matter of days, he informed the Powers-that-be that he was antagonistic towards people of one of the other nations partaking in the evaluation and was therefore not a good candidate to be a member of the Kestrel Evaluation Squadron. Much to my surprise, his excuse was accepted and so, on October 15, 1964, I set off alone to make my way to RAF West Raynham in the County of Norfolk. However, that was not the end of my relationship with

Vulcans, or of Waddington, although I would never actually be posted there again.

Shortly after my arrival at West Raynham, Pam was able to join me because we were provided with Married Quarter housing. Up to that time, we had still been living in the Mount Street flat, paying rent to Mr. Brownlow and trying to limit his electric coin meter's greedy appetite by swathing the bare hot water tank in blankets as insulation, but with only marginal success. Around that time, Geoff Supple, now married to Joan, was looking for a place to live and so they gladly took up residence in the flat but had similar experiences to ours with Mr. 'Scrooge' Brownlow.

My experiences with the Kestrel and the multi-national squadron at West Raynham have been chronicled in my book '*Kestrel Squadron*', so I will skip over that 15-month period of my RAF service and pick up on my return to Bomber Command on February 1, 1966.

As the Kestrel evaluation wound down, RAF personnel were invited to name the station to which they would prefer to be posted when the squadron was disbanded. I, of course, chose Waddington, but apparently the name was too long for some 'shiny arse' at the RAF Records Office to type out, so instead they posted me to RAF Scampton on the other side of Lincoln. Not only that, but instead of being directly in contact with the Scampton Vulcans, I was posted into the Electronics Squadron, housed in a glass-fronted building nicknamed the Gin Palace, although its proper name was the Electronics Centre. During my time at West Raynham, I had been promoted to the rank of corporal, so my working attire in the Gin Palace was an NCO's white dustcoat rather than the khaki coloured dustcoats worn by the airmen.

The Gin Palace housed the second line servicing facilities for all electrical and electronic trades. 'Second Line' means the servicing and repair of components removed from the Vulcans either for routine maintenance or because they had become unserviceable. The landing lamp described earlier is one example of components serviced by the Electrical Section, to which I belonged and which was housed in the Gin Palace. We also serviced and tested electrical alternators and multiple other pieces of aircraft electrical equipment. To be honest, I wasn't displeased with this particular assignment because it was, for the most part, an 8 to 5 job with only an occasional night shift when a junior NCO and airman needed to be present to deal with any urgent business that might arise, although it rarely did. In other words, it was a cushy number and I enjoyed the work, which mostly involved testing the alternators after they had been serviced by the airmen.

Although Scampton wasn't my preferred posting, it did have some attraction. It was the home of 617 Squadron, the famous Dambusters which was still based there but now equipped with the Vulcan Mk B2 instead of the equally famous Lancasters. The gate guardian, however, was a Lancaster on which a mocking quotation, attributed to Herman Goering, was emblazoned on its nose, "*No enemy plane will fly over the Reich territory.*" Guy Gibson's black Labrador's grave was and is still there on the lawn in front of one of the hangars. Sadly, the dog's name cannot be uttered in polite company, or printed here, because, in this modern era of political correctness, it is considered a racial slur. (It rhymes with the nickname for an Airframe tradesman). Back in Wing Commander Gibson's day, it was part of everyday language.

Scampton was also one of two stations whose V-bombers were equipped with the Blue Steel nuclear missile, but more about that later. When the station was first selected to be a Vulcan base, the runway needed to be extended to accommodate them, but the A15 road from Lincoln that runs past the station intersected the intended extension. The A15 is as straight as an arrow because it was built on the foundations of Ermine Street, the northern extension of that Roman road from Lincoln, so a bow-shaped curve was constructed at that location to divert the road around the end of the extended runway. On a map, the diversion has the appearance of a longbow of Robin Hood fame if one considers the original track of the A15 road to be the bowstring; therefore, the station badge was redesigned to incorporate a longbow and arrow, with the arrow pointing in the same direction, in relation to the bow, as that of the extended runway. Clever!

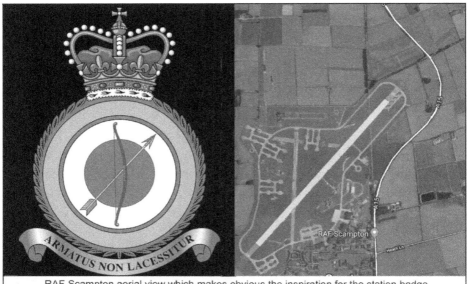

RAF Scampton aerial view which makes obvious the inspiration for the station badge "bow and arrow" motif.

Google Maps

Architecturally, the Gin Palace was identical to the Electronics Centres on all of the other V-bomber stations. It was a single storey, red brick building with a frontage that consisted mostly of tall glass windows. However, a grey, ugly building that was architecturally different had been jammed onto the end. It was a few feet taller than the existing building and constructed of grey corrugated material. This was the Blue Steel Missile Section and although it could be accessed from within the Gin Palace, that access was only permitted to those with the security clearance to be there, which neither I nor any of the other members of the Electrical Section possessed.

In the meantime, Pam and I still met socially with Stan and Dorothy Eilbeck and Johnny and Carol Thorne in continuation of the firm friendship we had forged with them, so my relationship with Waddington still existed in a social way. Both men had achieved the rank of Sergeant and although I was still a Corporal, Pam and I were invited as their guests in the Waddington Sergeants Mess almost every weekend.

Carol & Jonny Thorne, Pam & (author) Brian Carlin, Stan & Dorothy Eilbeck at some long-forgotten but evidently enjoyable event.

By this time, Stan and Johnny had both suffered through a 1-year unaccompanied tour in Borneo with its enforced separation from Dorothy and Carol. The question then was – when would it be my turn? I didn't have to wait too long for the answer to that question. In October 1966, I was on my way to RAF Labuan, an island offshore North Western mainland Borneo, where my friends Stan Eilbeck and Johnny Thorne had previously served, to do my duty in defending The Realm (and Malaysia) against President Sukarno during The Indonesian Confrontation. There was only one problem; the Confrontation had ended by this time but like a runaway locomotive, postings to the theatre of operations were still happening. Finally, someone at the Ministry of Defence must have gained a little common sense because those of us on Labuan who had served more than 6 months there were repatriated and those of us with less than that time had their postings changed to a normal 2½-year accompanied tour in Singapore. I, being in the latter category, spent only 2 months on Labuan before being posted to RAF Changi in Singapore on December 12, 1966. One month later, Pam arrived and we were able to set up home there. She had had to go back and live with her parents when my Labuan posting came through and so was delighted that we were back together again. However, our stay in Singapore couldn't be a 2½-year tour, because the end my 10-year engagement in the RAF was coming up on February 16, 1968 and exactly 6 months prior to the date of my impending demob, we were on a RAF Transport Command VC10, heading back to the U.K.

For my last posting, I could only request an area but not a specific station. This was the rule for anyone leaving the RAF, because theoretically, it would be the area in which a newly discharged serviceman would choose to settle in civilian life. I requested the Lincoln area, hoping that my posting would be to Waddington. My hopes were dashed, however when I learned that it was to be RAF Scampton once again. Not only that, but I found myself back in the Gin Palace, donning a white dustcoat in my old section as though I had never left. Many of the old faces were still there along with a few new ones. There were, however, two changes to the status quo that had occurred during my sojourn in the Far East. The first was that Bomber Command no longer existed; Bomber and Fighter commands had been combined into a new organization known as Strike Command.

What had also changed was that Electronics Centre personnel were now included in the manning of QRA. Prior to my overseas posting, those of us who worked in the Electronics Centre had escaped that irksome duty, but to be fair, we should have been included and someone somewhere must have come to the realization that the Gin Palace denizens were on a good thing.

Chapter 26: A Plan for the Future

With six months of my service remaining, my thoughts were occupied with finding a job in civilian life, but it soon became clear that an RAF electrical fitter, even if he was a Corporal, didn't make much of an impression on the 'Civvy Street' natives. Prospective employers wanted to know if I had an ONC or a City & Guilds, both of which are technical qualifications obtained by a course of study at a Technical College. But all I had to offer was my RAF training and two GCE 'O' levels, one in English and one in Maths. The only type of job offered to me was permanent night shift at a local power station. Not good – not good at all! Clearly, I needed some better civilian credentials, but how could I get them? I went to see the station Education Officer for advice on how to go about getting an ONC. He told me that it would mean going to the local technical college on a two year 'day release' course, but he also commented that I needed to have a GCE 'O' level in Physics, in addition to my two 'O' levels, before the college would accept me as a student.

Feeling very depressed by the Education Officer's counsel, I returned to the Electrical Section. Moping around, by chance I got into conversation with Frank, one of the airmen in the Section, and related to him what the Education Officer had told me. Frank, as it happened, was already taking a City & Guilds course at Lincoln College of Technology and was in his second year. He had a completely different opinion to that of the Education Officer and assured me that the College would gladly enrol me on the basis of my RAF service and the two 'O' levels. Not only that, but he advised me that the academic year had only just begun, so there was time for me to get enrolled for the current year and encouraged me to go and see the college Principal as soon as possible. Taking his advice, I hastily drove to the college and was granted an immediate interview with the Principal. He welcomed me and without further ado, enrolled me in the 2-year ONC Electrical & Electronics 'day release' course, but also cautioned that it would be hard work. Back at Scampton, my Flight Commander granted me permission to attend the course for one day a week (day release).

Realizing that leaving the service in just six months when the ONC course lasted for two years wasn't very practical, I applied to extend my service engagement for another two years. This too was granted. Attending those first course classes was difficult, as the college Principal had cautioned, but I had no option other than to work at it. Two years later, my efforts were rewarded with an Ordinary National Certificate in Electrical & Electronic Engineering. But during that intervening time, I was still in the RAF and continued with my service, including a few stints on QRA.

Chapter 27: QRA at Scampton

Although Scampton's QRA was subject to exactly the same alerts as Waddington and the other V-bomber stations, things were a little different because of the Blue Steel stand-off missiles with which the Scampton aircraft were armed.

When launched, the Blue Steel was propelled by highly volatile High Test Peroxide (HTP) that became explosive when mixed with kerosene, which acted as the catalyst. At Scampton, HTP scared the hell out of everyone who had anything to do with it. We were well educated in the fact that contact with the skin would cause immediate whitening, due to the production of oxygen below the skin and extensive burns would occur unless it was washed off in seconds. Contact with eyes could cause blindness. Because of its delightful characteristics, large ponds of water were located close to the QRA dispersal pans. Those of us working around the fuelled Blue Steel armed Vulcans on QRA were frequently reminded that if we came into contact with the ugly stuff, we were to make a beeline for the nearest pond and jump in, skipping the intermediate step of changing into our bathing trunks in the process.

Probably because of the volatile nature of HTP, Blue Steel armed aircraft never taxied during an alert exercise when the 'free-fall' V-bombers at other stations were commanded to do so. Therefore, the highest level of alert we ever experienced at Scampton was 'engine start'.

The danger of HTP leaking from the missiles meant that they needed to be closely and continuously monitored. There are no prizes for guessing who did the monitoring. Unlike Waddington where we could relax and have an uninterrupted night's sleep, absent an Exercise Edom alert, which didn't happen every day or night, part of the QRA ground crews' duties on the Scampton QRA was to patrol all three aircraft 24 hours a day, 7 days a week. One individual continuously walked around from aircraft to aircraft for one hour, during which time he was to pay close attention to the Blue Steel to confirm that there was no sign of anything leaking from it. If there was, he was supposed to report it immediately. Personally, I never saw any leaks, for which I am eternally grateful.

With only twelve ground crew manning the three QRA aircraft, the one-hour patrols came around twice for each person in a 24 hour period, which in most cases meant having to get out of bed at some unearthly hour and begin patrolling. The man coming off patrol had the duty of waking up his successor, often suffering all manner of colourful verbal abuse in the process.

Besides checking for HTP leaks, the man on patrol had one other duty to perform during his rounds of the aircraft. It was something that always struck me as being very 'low tech'. There was an electric heater somewhere in the bowels of the missile which was powered from a small transformer mounted up on the equipment ledge in the nose wheel bay. It seems that these transformers were prone to failure and if this happened it could cause some kind of unknown problem within the missile. To guard against any problem due to a failed transformer becoming serious, our other standing order was to reach up into the wheel bay and physically feel the transformer. If it was warm, all was well, but if it felt cool we were to alert the SNCO in charge of QRA immediately. Obviously, with a continuous patrol visiting each aircraft every few minutes, it wouldn't take very long for a failed transformer to be noticed.

***

One weekend while on QRA, following an 'engine start' Exercise Edom on the Sunday, I believe that I came as close as I ever did to finding myself on the carpet on a serious charge.

When the engines had been started, ground power was disconnected from all three Vulcans, as would happen for a normal sortie. At the end of the exercise, however, when ground power needed to be restored, the 28 volt DC ground power contactor, a large electrical contactor that mechanically latched closed when energized, failed to latch in on one of the aircraft. Two of us on that QRA shift were electricians; a Junior Technician from The Line and me, a Corporal from the Gin Palace. As the senior of the two, it was my responsibility to diagnose and rectify the fault. This being QRA, however, there was a limit on how long a Vulcan could be 'off line' because, in theory, we were at 15 minutes readiness and so all aircraft needed to be fully serviceable and ready to scramble within that short time period. In addition, it wasn't just a local matter – the Bomber Controller was immediately informed of the situation and we were given one hour to get the Vulcan back on line again. If we couldn't fix the problem in that time frame, another aircraft would have to be brought onto QRA, which meant a lot of work for a lot of people, not the least of which was de-fuelling the HTP from the retiring aircraft's Blue Steel and then removing the missile from that Vulcan and installing it on the replacement aircraft. HTP refuelling of the missile would then have to be performed to bring it up to readiness. Because of this, duty personnel throughout the station were put on readiness to bring a replacement Vulcan out to QRA. Talk about putting a little pressure on a couple of electricians!

My young J/T colleague was certain that the problem was a faulty contactor on the aircraft. I wasn't so sure. By this time, it had been four or five years since I had worked hands-on on a Vulcan, but something at the back of my mind niggled at me that this wasn't the first time that I had seen this problem and that it wasn't what it appeared to be. However, we phoned the office and requested that a new contactor be ordered on a V.O.G basis.

In the RAF, at that time, if an aircraft was grounded for need of a serviceable part, the part could be ordered on a priority basis known as A.O.G (Aircraft on the Ground). When initiated, a signal went out to the Supply Squadrons on all stations likely to hold the part and when located, the part was expeditiously transported to the station where the grounded aircraft was located. A similar but higher priority system was in place for V-bombers; this was known as V.O.G – (V-bomber on the Ground).

Having ordered a replacement contactor on a V.O.G priority, I told the J/T that we needed to go into the QRA office and take a look at the circuit diagram. He cockily insisted that it was the contactor on the aircraft, citing his 'experience' out on The Line. I could sense that he was contemptuous of me because in his eyes, I was just a know-nothing 'fairy' from the Gin Palace, not a tough, greasy-anorak wearing Line animal like him. Little did he realize that I had previously played the same role before trading my greasy anorak for a white dustcoat. Nor was I about to let him know that.

In the office, we looked at the appropriate circuit diagram. As I traced through the circuit, my suspicion that there was something else involved soon manifested itself. The circuit for the aircraft contactor was completed through the contacts of another contactor in the Ground Power Unit (GPU). Now, fully recalling my previous experience, I knew that there was an easy way to check the integrity of the GPU contactor. Motioning for the J/T to follow me back out to the aircraft and grabbing a screwdriver on the way, we headed back to the scene of the crime, while my cocky young companion continued to protest that it was a waste of time because he *just knew* the cause of the problem. When we arrived at the pan, I unplugged the power cable.

As with the aircraft of all NATO countries, the interface between the aircraft and the ground power systems is configured in what is known as a NATO plug and socket; the plug being on the aircraft and the socket on the end of the power cable from the GPU. The 28 volt cable socket consists of two large holes for the positive and negative sides of the circuit and a small socket that acts as a means of orienting the two larger sockets so that the correct polarity is achieved. But the small socket has another function; it is split into two halves which are electrically isolated from each other until they make contact with the corresponding small pin on the aircraft. In the case of the Vulcan, this completes the interlock circuit for the on-board contactor when the GPU contactor is energized closed.

Holding the power cable in one hand, I rammed the screwdriver into the small socket hole to simulate the small pin on the aircraft and then asked the J/T to push the 'on' button on the GPU. This should have caused the contactor on the GPU to energize closed and stay mechanically latched when he released the button, but that didn't happen. Instead, the contactor reopened as soon as he let it go; it wasn't latching. A look of surprise came over the J/T's face and dare I say, a reluctant realization that this 'fairy' corporal wasn't as ignorant of the Vulcan electrical system as he had assumed.

We were still within our hour of grace, so I quickly informed the Flight Sergeant in the office that the problem was the GPU. He arranged to have a spare GPU towed from a nearby vacant pan to replace the unserviceable one. We then fired it up, plugged it in and *voila* – it latched in and connected the 28 volts to the aircraft. On hearing the good news back at the office, the Flight Sergeant heaved a sigh of relief and then informed Operations, which then informed the Bomber Controller that the Vulcan was back on line. Next, the V.O.G. was cancelled although, by that time, a new contactor was probably on its way to the station stores.

The J/T said very little but I knew, or at least hoped, that he had learned something valuable from the incident. As for me, I felt that I had had a narrow escape. If we had gone ahead with the J/T's diagnosis and changed the aircraft contactor or, worse still, had allowed a replacement Vulcan to have been brought onto QRA, I am certain that I would have been for the high jump shortly afterwards when the real nature of the snag was discovered.

Blue Steel Standoff Nuclear Missile

Photo by Liftarn taken at the Midland Air Museum, Warwickshire, England.
https://commons.wikimedia.org/wiki/File:Avro_blue_steel_side_9m07.JPG#filehistory

Chapter 28: Odds and Ends

As we approach the end of this more or less chronological narrative, there are a few random items that might be of interest to the reader, but which don't fit too well into the main narrative, so I have gathered them here as odds and ends.

Tale of a Tail

There were a few and thankfully rare occasions when a Vulcan was known to assume the 'rotate' attitude, as though about to leap into the air but while perfectly stationary on the ground. These awkward and unwanted situations occurred because the aircraft's centre of gravity had been accidentally transferred too far to the rear when a partial fuel load was inadvertently allowed to migrate from the forward to the aft tanks.

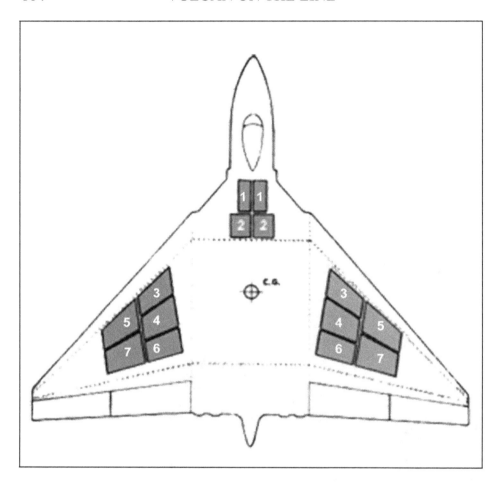

A Vulcan's fuel load was distributed between 14 interconnected tanks; seven of which were on the port side and an equal number on the starboard side in a similar but mirror-image configuration. The four largest volume tanks occupied the section of fuselage between the crew compartment and the bomb bay and squatted directly above the nose wheel. The weight of fuel in these four forward tanks, bearing down on the nose wheel, counterbalanced the weight of fuel in the ten aft tanks, all of which were in the aircraft's wings; three inboard on each side and two outboard.

During ground refuelling, fuel was automatically metered into the tanks on a sequenced basis in such way that the fuel in each tank was always maintained at the same percentage as that in all the other tanks, relative to each tank's volume. For example, when one tank became half full, all tanks became half full, regardless of the volume of fuel in the tank. This ensured that the Centre of Gravity (CG) of the total fuel load always remained forward of the Vulcan's airframe CG. This was necessary because the aircraft's attitude, when resting on its undercarriage, sloped downwards from front to rear; more pronounced on the B1 and B1A versions, but still evident on the B2. If the fuel CG moved aft of the airframe CG, the Vulcan would tend to become tail heavy – a situation that was to be avoided at all costs, although on a few rare occasions Murphy's Law struck and tossed the proverbial spanner into the works.

The main culprit was the In-Flight Refuelling System, which, unlike the slow, carefully choreographed ground refuelling system, required that the operation of transferring fuel from the tanker aircraft to the receiving Vulcan needed to be implemented in the shortest possible time.

The In-Flight Refuelling operation was initiated by operating a Master Switch on the co-pilot's side console. This caused all fuel tank valves to open simultaneously so that the incoming fuel flowed into all of the receiving Vulcan's tanks as rapidly as possible, thereby minimising the length of time that tanker and receiving aircraft needed to maintain their probe-to-drogue connection. The co-pilot manually maintained the aircraft's centre of gravity, or trim, during this operation by transferring fuel to various tanks fore or aft and port or starboard, as needed, by means of dedicated CG transfer pumps.

On the rare occasions that a Vulcan was tipped onto its tail, it was probably due to the In-Flight Refuelling System Master Switch being operated when the fuel tanks were less than full. Because all of the fuel valves opened when this happened, the fuel in the forward tanks flowed downhill into the rear wing tanks, shifting the CG to the rear. When there was sufficient weight of fuel in the rear to overcome the weight of the forward section, the nose rose, the tail dipped and the aircraft rotated around the axis of the main undercarriage until its aft end made contact with the ground.

This happened very rarely, mainly because it was standard practice to refuel the aircraft to 100% of its fuel capacity after it had landed, so if the In-Flight Refuelling Master Switch was operated, accidentally or on purpose, the fuel would have nowhere to go because all aft tanks were already full. But then there were those rare occasions.

Geoff Supple remembers one incident well, because he was a member of the party of 'volunteers' that helped to man-handle the Vulcan back onto all three sets of its wheels.

It happened around December one year, on the Bravo dispersal at Waddington – the one adjacent to the A15 Lincoln-to-Sleaford road, which must have been quite a strange sight for passing motorists. Maybe some thought it was being readied for rocket launching. Geoff says that some wag suggested that a VTOL Vulcan photo would have been a top seller as a Christmas card.

His recollection is that the in-flight refuelling probe was being tested for functionality and leaks by using it to refuel the Vulcan. There would have been a right way and a wrong way to do this. Apparently, the fuelling crew selected the latter option. The right way would have included picketing the aircraft, so that the nose wheel would have been held firmly on the ground.

It also seems that whoever sat in the pilot's seat, supposedly monitoring the refuelling operation, failed to notice that anything was amiss and when sufficient fuel had migrated to the aft tanks to bias the CG far enough aft, the nose of the Vulcan rose in stately slow motion until the ECM pod at the aircraft's extreme aft end came to rest on the concrete surface of the pan.

Geoff did not witness it actually happening, having been summoned on the double, with several other ground crew, to somehow restore the Vulcan back to equilibrium. So one can only imagine the Keystone Cops chaos that must have ensued when the event was occurring. With the nose wheel now 6 or 7 feet above ground level, the man in the cockpit would have found himself in a precarious position as would any other ground crew members who might also have been in there. The bottom rung of the crew entrance ladder would have been several feet off the ground – too high for anyone to jump from. Possibly a Safety Raiser was brought over and raised until it was at a height where the unfortunate man could step onto it and then be lowered to the ground.

The Crew Chief and other senior NCOs then must have spent some time scratching their heads, fearing that there might be serious structural damage to the Vulcan and that it would have to be written off. As early evening rolled around, Bravo dispersal attracted everyone and his dog, all proffering solutions to solve the problem of getting the Vulcan back safely and completely on its three legs. Geoff and his fellow motley crew members, having been detailed as the muscle power for whatever solution proved most suitable, had also arrived and stood around waiting for The Plan to be hatched, although not being shy at offering their own suggestions.

Eventually, some time after a decision had been made, a lorry arrived carrying a load of railway sleepers, obtained from God knows where. These were then stacked directly under the nose wheel. So far, so good!

The fuel bowser was then pressed into service and began defuelling the Vulcan – at least the Refuelling Power Pack in the port main undercarriage bay was accessible, otherwise this operation would have been difficult. Meanwhile, a crew from the Fire Section turned up, bringing with them a number of fire hoses, which, with the aid of a Giraffe (a long, tall stairway-on-wheels contraption) they draped over the nose of the Vulcan so that the ends hung down on either side, within reach of the ground crew. This is where Geoff and his mates came in. Teams of men got on either side and grabbed on to the ends of the fire hoses and held on to them. Meanwhile, as fuel was pumped out of the aircraft and into the bowser, the nose began to lower. The fire hose crew's job was to hold on to the hoses in case there was a sudden movement in the opposite direction and to stabilize the nose as it descended. As the nose wheel was just about to make contact with the first railway sleeper, the sleeper was removed. All in all, this was a controlled return of the nose wheel to terra firma.

All of this pantomime was in full view of motorists, mostly civilians, driving along the A15. Conversations within the privacy of some of the cars can only be imagined.

"I say Doris, whatever are those air force chappies up to over there?"

"Do you think they're trying to climb up onto that plane, dear?"

"I don't know what they're up to. Maybe it's some kind of initiative test."

The defuelling process continued for a long time; the nose being brought down carefully, inch by inch with a sleeper being removed each time the nose wheel came close to contacting it, until the Vulcan finally stood on its three sets of wheels.

No doubt a thorough structural inspection of the hapless Vulcan followed in the coming days, while a Board of Inquiry was, in all probability, convened to determine the cause of the accident, point fingers at the responsible party or parties and make recommendations in the interest of preventing future similar occurrences. One likely outcome was that one or more individuals found his promising RAF career nipped in the bud. As for making 'recommendations in the interest of preventing future similar occurrences' – whatever those might have been, they failed in their intent, because it did happen again on a few other occasions, two of those being at Goose Bay in Canada.

Trade nicknames

Besides their proper names, most trades had nicknames by which other trades referred to them.

Engines technicians were known as Engine Bashers to all and sundry. Some people also called them 'Sooties' at Waddington, because they were covered in soot after climbing into Vulcan engine jet pipes and then having to crawl up their full length to inspect for cracks and damage to the rear turbine blades.

Airframes were known as 'Riggers', a time-honoured nickname that harked back to the early days of flight when aircraft wings were supported by wire cables that needed to be rigged. The airframes tradesmen were the direct descendents of those old-time Riggers and so the name was retained as a nickname. Theirs was a job that demanded more muscle power than most other trades so they were, at times, referred to as 'Heavies' (a moniker that was also applied to the Engines tradesmen for a similar reason). One of the Airframes' frequent tasks was to change wheels when enough rubber had burned off the tyres during landings. On the Line, they didn't use the 'Up one' technique; that was used only when the entire aircraft needed to be raised off the ground. Instead they used a solid, clunky piece of steel equipment know as a Gooseneck and a hydraulic bottle jack that, when used together, could raise an individual wheel off the ground.

Instruments were also 'Bashers' – Instrument Bashers; rather unkind because they had the job of dealing with the most delicate of equipment.

Radio and Radar were collectively referred to as 'Fairies'. Don't shoot the messenger; that's what they were really called by all others.

Armourers were known as 'Plumbers'. I never found out how they came by this nickname.

Electricians: the others referred to us as by two names. Leckies (plural, i.e. a Shock of Electricians) was the most common throughout the RAF. A single individual was a Lecky. But some of the other trades referred to us as 'Light Heavies' at Waddington. We needed some muscle power to lift some of the weightier components from high up locations, but it was also something of a pun, since we tended to all of the lighting on the aircraft.

Pee tubes and Ration Heaters

Sanitary arrangements on the Vulcan can, at best, be described as primitive. The only concession to the relief of the call of nature was a rubber bladder, not unlike a Rugby football bladder, that hung from a clip at each crewmember's station. In its unused state, the bladder was designed to be a flat, oval shape, having a number of pleats that would allow it to expand as the need arose. The bladder was topped by a chromed metal cup wide enough to accommodate a stallion's appendage and certainly large enough to accept the most generously endowed human user. A hinged lid closed the cup when not in use. The lower part of the cup narrowed down to mate with the rubber bladder. A plastic screw-in plug at the bottom of the bladder enabled it to be emptied of its contents at the end of the sortie, although this needed to be performed in a most careful manner to avoid the emptier's hands or clothing from accidentally coming into contact with the fluidic contents during the operation. Sometimes the plug wasn't properly reinserted, resulting in a messy 'accident' the next time the pee tube was used in flight. The whole ensemble was informally referred to as a 'pee tube'.

The pee tube was a last resort. Most aircrew made damned sure that their biological bladders were as empty as possible before climbing aboard their Vulcan. Indeed, it was quite common to see a flight-suited individual watering the grass at the edge of the pan prior to climbing aboard. Using the tube was not easy because of the layers of flight clothing worn by the aircrew – garments such as an air ventilated suits worn underneath the flight suit. It was virtually impossible to use it sitting down, not to mention the cramped conditions in the Vulcan cabin, so unstrapping oneself from the seat then moving to a relatively open area was a necessity. It was even worse for the pilots, who would have needed to extricate themselves from a live ejection seat and then negotiate their way down the flight deck ladder. Consequently, the pee tubes were used only on rare occasions.

The job of emptying and cleaning them was laid at the feet of the Airframes airman as part of his Post Flight servicing procedure, but typically any aircrew member who had had the doubtful pleasure of using the pee tube in flight usually emptied his own at the edge of the pan, although this was not always the case. The preferred method was just to upend the device and let the contents empty from the cup end. Removing the plug, as mentioned before, was fraught with peril. Even if the user emptied his own pee tube, the Airframes man was still saddled with the responsibility of washing it out, which was not exactly a pleasant task.

I am not aware of any arrangements should an aircrew member have been in dire need of a 'number two'. The pee tube certainly would not have been suitable for such an undertaking and anyone needing to heed that particular call of nature would have had to sit on it until his return to terra firma. Significantly during the Falklands operation, when the flying time was projected to last several times longer than the typical Cold War sortie, a chemical toilet was installed on board as an essential piece of equipment (reference: 'Vulcan 607' by Rowland White).

The Vulcan also lacked a galley and so the only concession to a hot meal was a soup tin heater at each crewmember's station. It was approximately the height of a soup tin but the wall in which the heating element resided was thicker – probably about half an inch if memory serves me right. After the soup can was inserted, a metal strap was fitted across the top, presumably to prevent the can from escaping from the heater's clutches. That was the only hot food available to the crew, however they usually brought along tasty French rolls filled with very nice ingredients that made our ground crew mouths water, but it was a case of Officers, for the Use Of. Rarely were there any leftovers to be greedily consumed by we bottom dwellers.

Air brakes

The big, oblong air brake paddles that sprouted from above and below the Vulcan's wing roots, to slow down its forward momentum when landing, were extended and retracted by two powerful electric motors located in the bomb bay. Both motors were coupled to a common gearbox which then drove the mechanical linkage to operate the air brakes. There's an interesting little story about those motors.

The motor-gearbox assembly was arranged in such a way that the gearbox was in the centre with the motors coupled to it on either side. Picture the rear axle arrangement of a car with the differential gear in the centre and two stub axles coming out on either side. The air brake gearbox arrangement was similar, except that the two electric motors were connected to the gearbox instead of the car's drive shaft. Because they were opposed at 180° to each other, the motors rotated in opposite directions; one clockwise and the other anticlockwise. Think about it – the wheels on the left side of a car rotate anticlockwise while those on the right side turn clockwise. The stub axles from the air brake gearbox rotated in a similar way; one anticlockwise and one clockwise, therefore the motors did likewise. That, of course was for one operation, let's say to extend the air brakes. The motors were then electrically reversed to retract the air brakes, which meant that all elements now rotated in the opposite direction.

Like most electrical and electronic devices on aircraft, the power connections to the motors were by means of screwed plugs and sockets. The socket for each motor was at the end of an electrical cable, one cable per motor, while its corresponding plug was a fixture on the motor housings.

During one particular Major servicing operation in the hangar, during which the aircraft was taken almost completely apart so that all of its components could be inspected and serviced, the air brake motors were disconnected and removed for servicing in the Electrical Bay. When they were reinstalled several weeks later, it was at that point that the infamous Murphy's Law struck with a vengeance. In this context, the law could be stated as, *'Anything that can be done wrong will be done wrong'*.

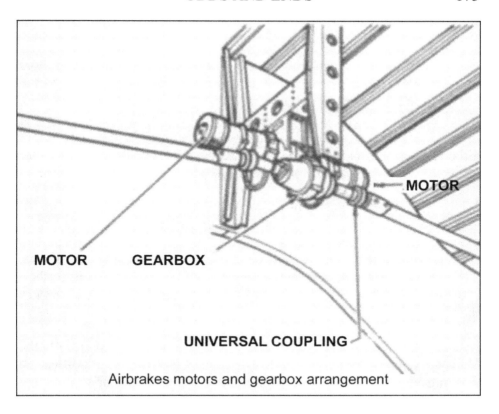

MOTOR

MOTOR   **GEARBOX**

UNIVERSAL COUPLING

Airbrakes motors and gearbox arrangement

The electrical tradesman tasked with reconnecting the motors unfortunately connected the starboard motor's electrical socket to the port motor plug and vice versa. An NCO would have inspected the installation and over-signed on the aircraft's Form 700 to confirm that it had been done correctly. That, however, was just for the installation, although both individuals either misread the cable identification marker sleeves, or the sleeves were mislabelled.

Later, when electrical power was restored to the Vulcan and it was time to perform a functional test, the air brakes were selected to extend. Unfortunately, because the cross-connected motors rotated in the opposite directions to that which was required, the air brakes, although already fully retracted, now tried to retract even further, causing considerable damage to the airframe and the brakes themselves.

This mishap occurred during the very early years of the Vulcan's operational service and very quickly thereafter, a modification was introduced to change the orientation of each motor's plug and socket connection. In other words, the alignment of keyways on the plug shells that corresponded to those on socket shells were arranged so that they could only be mated when the correct cable was introduced to the correct plug. The modification prevented further similar misfortunes occurring with the air brakes.

Brake chute

While on the subject of braking and eventually bringing several tons of a hurtling Vulcan to a halt, the pilot had the option of streaming the brake parachute in addition to applying the wheel brakes. As soon as all undercarriage wheels were on the runway, he could operate the brake chute switch, whereupon a solenoid operated latch at the rear end of the brake chute compartment, atop the bulbous ECM pod, released the brake chute door, allowing a powerful spring to force it rapidly upwards. A small drogue chute then pulled the main brake chute out behind the Vulcan, where its ribbed canopy opened in the form of an oversized mushroom that blossomed out behind the aircraft, exerting a powerful retarding force that helped to save the wheel brakes from overheating. When the aircraft slowed to an acceptable speed, another cockpit-initiated action caused the shackle device holding the parachute lines to release. The chute then collapsed in billowing folds onto the runway from where a waiting Land Rover crew quickly gathered it up and took it off to the Safety Equipment Section, where it was inspected, serviced and repacked, ready for use in another Vulcan.

Meanwhile, the Vulcan continued on, eventually slowing down to taxiing speed. The brake chute door remained in its wide open state because there was no mechanism to re-close it. That operation was performed manually after another brake parachute was installed.

James Hancock Photography

The replacement parachute pack was as long as a grown man and very heavy. It needed to be man-handled into the brake chute compartment atop the ECM pod. This task was undertaken by a couple of Safety Equipment workers, using a safety raiser to elevate the chute pack up to the level of compartment, or sometimes a Giraffe. It was then a wrestling match to manoeuvre the pack into the compartment, laying it out so that it was flat and then connecting the line shackle to the brake chute release mechanism. That done, all that remained was to close the compartment door by compressing the powerful spring that held it open. No task for mere human muscle power; this required the help of screw jack, one end of which attached to strong point on the ECM pod and the other end to a lip on the end of the door. From there, it was a case of winding the wheel of the screw jack around seemingly countless times until the door latched closed, ready to be released during the next brake chute deployment.

Closing the brake chute door.

Brake fires

Vulcan pilots didn't always deploy the brake chute, relying instead on the aerodynamic braking, courtesy of the large surface area of the aircraft's delta shape which was held up at a steep angle towards the direction of travel for as long as possible. That, coupled with the wheel brakes could reduce the initial landing speed to taxiing speed by the time the Vulcan reached the end of the runway. Often though, the wheel brakes on all sixteen wheels of the main undercarriage became overheated to the point of being on fire. For this reason, a Fire Section Land Rover was stationed at the end of the runway when a Vulcan was due to land. When the aircraft reached the end of the runway, it would come to a halt and then a Fireman would emerge from the Land Rover to walk around the undercarriage and perform a visual inspection. If he perceived a brake fire, a dry powder chemical fire extinguisher was brought from the Land Rover and sprayed on the brakes to quell the fire. The reason dry powder was used is because a liquid medium would suddenly chill the hot metal of the brake components and possibly cause distortion or fracturing of some parts.

Western Rangers

I was never fortunate enough to get a flight in a Vulcan, although my good friend Stan Eilbeck was lucky enough to be included as a supernumerary crew member on a Western Ranger exercise. That particular exercise involved a flight to Offut USAF Air Force Base in America, staging through the Canadian Defence Force base at Goose Bay, Labrador.

A Vulcan's Crew Chief typically flew as an extra crew member on these exercises, because he was needed to supervise refuelling and servicing during the trip. He also needed to be able to diagnose and rectify any minor snags that would almost certainly crop up during the trip. Most Crew Chiefs were cross-trained on all trades, giving them the ability to deal with this requirement, but some, whose basic trade was Airframes or Engines, were a little less confident in their abilities when it came to electrical snags, which were arguably the most likely to manifest themselves. To counteract their deficiency, many would request that an electrical technician also be included as a seventh member of the crew, which is why Stan was selected for this particular Western Ranger.

The Vulcan crew cabin included two extra seats, named the 6th and 7th seats for obvious reasons. They were little more than a thick foam cushion on top of a wooden box with another similar cushion as a backrest. These were down in the well of the crew cabin, facing each other from opposing bulkheads. There were no windows and little light, so the trip of several hours could be quite boring. Occasionally, Stan was able to crawl into the bomb aimer's prone position to look out of the bomb aimer's window, but there's not too much to see travelling across the Atlantic.

Since the aircraft intercom was the means by which the crew talked to each other, Stan and the Crew Chief were able to listen in on the conversations and to the ground to air communications. Chatting about his trip when he returned, Stan recalled that, at one point, the Vulcan contacted a weather ship somewhere over the Atlantic. The radio operator on the ship asked the Vulcan pilot for identification, but the pilot only responded that it was a 'four-engine jet' and would not provide any further information.

The crew members of that particular Vulcan flight were shocked to discover, on arriving back at Waddington, that while they were re-crossing the Atlantic on their return journey, US President John F. Kennedy had been assassinated.

Thunderball

The James Bond film *Thunderball* featured a nuclear armed Vulcan that is hi-jacked by the bad guys so that they can use the warheads to blackmail NATO by threatening to explode them in a major city, which turns out to be Miami, Florida. In the film, the 'airbase' on which the hi-jacking takes place is supposed to be in the south of England, but in fact the Vulcan sequences were filmed in the East Midlands at Waddington and featured two Waddington B1A aircraft. That is until remarkably accurate scale models were substituted for the real thing in later sequences.

The filming took place in 1965, which was also the same year that the film was released. I first saw it in 1966 while stationed in Singapore, two years after I had been posted from Waddington, so never witnessed any of the filming first-hand, but heard some comments in later years from some of the people who were there.

In full disclosure, because it was such a long time ago since I first watched the film and although I remembered some of the Vulcan sequences, it seemed only fair to view it again in order to comment on it. For that reason, I recently purchased a DVD of *Thunderball* that I found on eBay.

The Waddington sequences on the ground and in the air were, for the purposes of the story, all supposed to be at night, but were actually shot during the day using filters to imply darkness. To go along with the illusion, the crew coach bringing the aircrew to the Vulcan has its headlights turned on; the inward facing sodium lamps around the aircraft pans were illuminated. Also, when taking off, the scrambling Vulcans had their landing lamps turned on – something that never happened in real life. After all, they're 'landing' lamps, not 'take-off' lamps.

The story also supposed that the hi-jacking pilot was a member of the French air force and that he had been invited to accompany the crew on board as a guest during a NATO exercise, but he was an impostor planted by the bad guys in place of the real French pilot.

Four of the Line Squadron lads taking a break during the filming of the *Thunderball* Vulcan sequence. L - R (Unidentified), George Chinnery, Alan Hewitt, Bill Aitken.
Photo courtesy of George Chinnery.

The shot of the crew boarding the Vulcan was filmed on the ORP with three other Vulcans in the background, because the 'NATO exercise' apparently included a four-Vulcan scramble. The 'star' Vulcan's starter crew all wore white overalls, as did the crews that could be seen in the background moving around the other ORP aircraft. That would not have been normal for an exercise; white overalls were worn only for VIP or Open Day scramble demonstrations. Although in a way, this was a scramble demonstration because it would be seen by a much wider audience than would ever be present for a Waddington Open Day.

To anyone familiar with Vulcans, however, there were several other flubs and departures from reality. A sharp-eyed viewer might have noticed that the Vulcan being boarded on the ORP was XA913 because its tail number was also stencilled on the main undercarriage door and clearly visible in the background as the crew climbed on board, assisted by the white-overalled Crew Chief. Later, during the aerial shots, the number XH506 was clearly visible on the tailfin.

In the V-force, it was an article of faith that V-bombers *never* flew with armed nuclear weapons aboard; the only exception being the Valiants that dropped nuclear test weapons during Operation Grapple. Operationally, the only time that V-bombers would carry an armed weapon was if they were making a one-way flight to deliver it to the enemy, which thankfully never happened. Therefore, had this been real life, the hi-jacked Vulcan would not have carried nuclear weapons on a NATO exercise. And speaking of weapons; the aircraft was configured to carry only one large nuclear weapon which occupied most of the bomb bay, not the two weapons featured in the film. I had to chuckle when I saw that one of the nukes had 'Handle like eggs' stencilled on its casing. In fact, this directive appeared on an electronic black box which may have been noticed by the film crew (I don't recall what the box was, but seem to think it was within the Instrument trade's realm of responsibility).

During the flight, the guest pilot is initially sitting on a 6th seat, which is positioned behind the rear crew members instead of against the cabin bulkhead in the well of the crew compartment, where it is below the level of the rear crew members. The cabin area surrounding the rear crew seems reasonably authentic, until one notices an 'emergency exit' on the bulkhead next to the Nav Radar. In fact, the only emergency exit for those members was through the cabin entrance hatch. At this point, the AEO and Nav Plotter are wearing their oxygen masks but the Nav Radar's mask is dangling loose.

The Captain then invites the guest to change places with the co-pilot, which both proceed to do. Shortly afterwards, the guest pilot unplugs his oxygen supply hose from the aircraft system and connects it to a special oxygen unit that he has smuggled on board. He then inserts a small poison gas capsule into a receptacle on the co-pilot's side console. Immediately, all of the crew members die from breathing the poison gas through their oxygen masks. Realistically, killing the crew in this manner is simply impossible. In the process of performing his dastardly deed, the impostor depressurizes the cabin and from then onwards a giant red light on the cockpit coaming flashes on and off. There was no such large warning light in a real Vulcan cockpit.

After a few air to air and flyover shots, the filming resorts to models when the Vulcan plays ducks and drakes on the ocean surface before sinking in the shallow water just off the Bahamas. How the hell did it get there? The Bahamas is over 4,000 miles from England while the Vulcan's Mk B1A's range was just 2,600 miles, (the B2 could fly 4,000 miles, but this was definitely a B1A Vulcan).

Those are just a few examples of the celluloid crowd playing fast and loose with the facts, but they saved the *pièce de résistance* for last. James Bond discovers the Vulcan in its sub-surface hiding place, so he rents some scuba gear and swims down to it and into the open bomb bay. Lo and behold, he finds a door in the forward bulkhead of the bomb bay that leads directly into the crew compartment where he finds the dead crew. There's just one tiny problem with this scenario; the forward bulkhead of the bomb bay does not incorporate a door and if there was, it would lead directly into the forward fuel tanks. And, if he got through there, he would be confronted with an impassable pressure bulkhead that isolates the pressurized crew compartment from the rest of the unpressurized Vulcan.

The film is fun to watch and in the author's humble opinion, one of the best James Bond films of them all, but to be able to enjoy it, Vulcan *cognoscenti* need to indulge in suspension of their disbelief, otherwise *Thunderball* could be better titled *Thunderbull*.

James Bond about to enter the supposed door from the bomb bay into the crew compartment in the Thunderball film.

United Artists Corporation and DanJaq LLC

Forward bulkhead of the Vulcan bomb bay as it really is. Look! No door!

Chapter 29: All Good Things...

In the year 1970, the Royal Navy Polaris submarine fleet took over the role of the British Nuclear Deterrent. A friend in the Missile Section confided that when the transfer had taken place, Denis Healey, the then Labour Party Minister of Defence, ordered that all of the Blue Steel inertial guidance systems be smashed to smithereens with sledge hammers so that they could never be used again. One wonders at the motives of former Communist Party member Mr. Healey. Was he making sure his friends in the USSR would never have to fear an attack by the Blue Steel, even if there was a future change of governing party? This was a travesty! The inertial guidance system on the missile was more advanced and accurate than the Vulcan's own NBS system and was a very high cost item. Some years later while working in Saudi Arabia, my then employer, ARAMCO operated a fleet of aircraft that were used to access remote sites. I often flew to some sites in one of the De Havilland Twin Otters, which used an inertial navigation system to get it to the exact location. One of the pilots told me that system cost more than the Otter itself. Just imagine how useful this system would have been if it had been available for the Black Buck operation to the Falklands so many years later.

***

On February 16th 1971, I became a civilian after having reached the exalted rank of sergeant during the second year of my extended engagement. Now, armed with an ONC, I was able to get a good job with a Lincoln firm as an electrical draughtsman. Pam and I had bought a bungalow in the local village of Cherry Willingham on our repatriation from Singapore and it happened to be directly below the approach flight path to Waddington's runway 21. Often I would look up at the stately delta wing shape of an overhead Vulcan as it passed a few thousand feet above me on its way to touch down and then watched its smoky trail as it faded into a speck in the distance. At times like that, I felt proud and privileged to have worked on such elegant aircraft.

This ends my narrative, but if you read on you will find two 'bonus' chapters on the following pages. The first is by my friend and former 'Line Animal' colleague, Geoff Supple. In his bonus chapter, Geoff humorously describes his and some of his fellow impoverished airmen's efforts to earn a little extra cash to support their young families by moonlighting in various interesting jobs.

The second bonus chapter is taken from a couple of posts by Tom McCormick that I came across on the PPrune – 'Did you fly the Vulcan' website (https://www.pprune.org/aviation-history-nostalgia/111797-did-you-fly-vulcan-merged.html). He was a Ground Electrician who was posted to Scampton around the same time that I was there on my second tour, although we never actually met while we were there. His recollections of maintaining Blue Steel test equipment and transporters caught my eye, as did his recollections of his posting to Goose Bay in the frigid northern reaches of Canada. Goose Bay is where our Vulcans first touched down to refuel (and probably for the crew to enjoy the relief of visiting a proper toilet) after crossing the Atlantic on various exercises and visits to USAF bases in America. Tom provides a very telling description of what it was like to serve there. I contacted him and obtained his permission to reproduce his posts, so Bonus Chapter 2 is a lightly edited version of his posts with some additional content that he included in his correspondence.

As for me, if you have read this far, I thank you for your interest and hope that you have enjoyed reading this book as much as I have enjoyed writing it.

Brian Carlin
San Diego, USA
1 March 2019

Bonus Chapter 1: Moonlighting

by

Geoff Supple

Moonlighting - the practice of holding a second regular job in addition to one's main job.

Prior to the 1964 Trade Structure righting a few wrongs, Servicemen, particularly those in the lower ranks were not well paid. Hence a young airman may well have considered moonlighting as a way of supplementing his income. Officially one was obliged to request permission to work part time or shift work from the Commanding Officer. This rarely happened and a blind eye was turned to serving members of the Armed Forces who manned Bars or drove Taxis to earn a few extra bob.

Some people worked shifts and so it was possible, say, for an RAF driver holding an HGV licence to moonlight for a local Haulier. It was also whispered around that a Chicken Processing and Packaging Plant in Lincoln employed many RAF personnel. In fact, rumour had it that a Klaxon was sounded at Swift's Butterball Chickens when a Mickey Finn exercise was about to be called.

I never put my hand to Packaging Chickens, but I certainly helped the local economy out at a few other Establishments. We had quite a lot of annual leave but unfortunately not the *do-re-mi* to venture on overseas holidays, so some extra income never went amiss. I recall stacking roofing timbers at Jewson's woodyard in Lincoln as well as grading and canning peas at Morrells in Bardney. These were both interesting experiences, but in truth could not hold a candle to the work I did for John Bullen at his Grantham Scrapyard.

It was officially named the Lincolnshire Processed Scrap Metal Company and the yard was in Grantham. Johnny Bullen's was known to RAF moonlighters the length and breadth of the county. John ran the yard with a few family members, some of the travelling community and any RAF lad who turned up on any given day and was prepared to graft for 4 shillings an hour in 1965. John was the last of a few and could best be described as eccentric. He ruled the yard with an iron hand (excuse the pun) and demanded an energetic pace from Dawn to Dusk. John was always fair, particularly with us RAF lads. If he had a good week he would sometimes give everyone a bonus. The nature of the trade saw the yard visited by characters from both sides of the law. Nobody messed with John; even the CID would roll up in pairs and be very respectful. Regulars were in awe of JB and spoke of the time that he had an altercation with a Big Gypsy Guy and offered to fight him stripped to the waist on the weigh bridge. I'm not sure if axes were involved but the Romany backed down and John booted him out of the yard.

Casual Labour was the term given to this sort of work. **No names, no N.I., no Income tax**, here today …. gone tomorrow. However, there was nothing casual about the work. I have never worked so hard, and it's no wonder that several moonlighters perhaps expecting an easier time didn't show up for Day 2.

A few times when I worked at the scrapyard, we stayed with my in-laws in Grantham. At other times, I can recall travelling from Waddington on the scooter one cold winter for a week and working from 7am until 6pm. *And if you tell that to the kids of today, they won't believe you.* Work usually began at 7 am with cable being dragged from a still smouldering bonfire. The insulation had been burned off overnight and this was followed by separating the copper, the aluminium and the steel wire armour. We still hadn't been working an hour and already we looked like Victorian Chimney Sweeps. By 8 am John would arrive and would begin to focus both the permanent staff and us guys in his own inimitable way. This usually entailed numerous expletives, changes of plan and several reminders that we weren't going to have him in the **Poor House** *that* day.

Another job we had was breaking up the Lead Acid Car batteries that had accumulated (again, excuse the pun) over the previous few days. Armed with a huge axe you would roll the battery on to its top, hit it an almighty crack along the bottom of the Bakelite casing, a couple more hefts with the axe to crack the ends followed by a sharp blow which would leave the plates free from the case. All this happened whilst another axe man behind you was doing the same thing, with the dilute sulphuric acid spraying all over the shop. The Lead (along with any mud or dust from the yard) was then shovelled into diggers and dropped into wagons bound for Paint factories. Not a Health and Safety Representative to be seen within miles.

Vacuum cleaners were *cleaned* for the aluminium blades and the copper from the motors. Rags and Woollens were sorted for quality. Metals were graded and loaded into Gunny Sacks. Sometimes the contents of the sacks were of dubious metallic composition, some *bad* topped up with some *good*. Standard practice if the yard was having a bad week, allegedly.

At the end of the day the Lorries bound for Sheffield were loaded with sacks of Copper of various grades, Brass, Bronze, Gunmetal, Aluminium, Steel and Cast. This was heavy work dragging the sacks and then somehow muscling them into the wagons.

Loading the sacks of rags onto the wagons was not the most pleasant of jobs as the rat population of the yard seemed to reside in this area, but there was a couple of Jack Russells that got their daily sport chasing the rodents across the yard.

At 6pm you clocked off, went home shattered, had a bath and an evening meal. If you weren't too knackered and the acid hadn't reduced your jeans to shreds you were up for another day at the scrapyard.

Friday was pay day. John appeared with the pay packets and called the names…. Donald Duck, Mickey Mouse etc it sounded like the cast from a Disney Movie.

I also turned my hand to other things. A 'one off' job, which paid well, was sweeping the runway at Waddington. I jest not! Contractors had resurfaced the runway and done a mechanical sweep but still weren't satisfied, so they recruited us guys. On the Saturday, hordes of us armed with wide brushes swept the runway and were paid a nice rate, thank-you very much.

An Ulsterman who lived near me in married quarters asked me if I'd like to do a bit of farm work over near Horncastle for a few evenings. Three of us went over after work and the farmer set us to work. We had to stack hay bales 4x4x4, the old-fashioned shape bales. I think from memory he paid us 1/3d a stack. We really moved across the field(s) and both parties were pleased.

The reason Paddy knew the farmer was they were both into playing the pipes. He was in the Waddington Pipe Band and the farmer was a supporter who got to play on the civilian gigs. I forgot to mention the farmer was a Scot, a generous one though!

When we'd finished stacking for the evening the farmer's wife would give us a beer and a sandwich. Meanwhile the two Pipers would march up and down the farmyard playing Flower of Scotland! Bizarre or what?

I started a Football Pools round, which just involved 3 hours work on a Thursday evening collecting round quarters. I canvassed and built up the round and very quickly, I was earning £8 commission with people paying me their section syndicate monies. Tax free, of course. When I got posted loads of guys were saying they would like to take the round over, so I sold it to a Ch/Tech Armourer for £32.

All in all, tough work and good times; I earned a few extra pounds and learned some life lessons.

Bonus Chapter 2: From Blue Steel to Goose Bay

by

Tom McCormick

September 1968 saw me, a fresh faced 18-year old Halton brat posted to RAF Scampton. But I should have known all was not straightforward when the level of Security Clearance needed caused me to have to wait an extra two months at Halton before I could take up my post at Scampton.

On joining the RAF and having been accepted for a Halton apprenticeship, I thought I was being clever in choosing the trade of Ground Electrician – it seemed to cover such a wide range of skills and thus seemed more interesting than 'just' Airframes or Engines. Little did I know that it was a passport to one of the hardest working trades in the whole of the RAF. Whereas those in the Black Hand Gang were focused on seeing off their aircraft and then either sleeping, playing cards or sport until they came back. I, on the other hand, was lumbered with a never ending stream of kit to be fixed. It ranged from domestic kettles and washing machines through aircraft ground power generating sets, inverters, MT and specialist vehicles to Palouste aircraft starter carts. In fact it was anything that was vaguely electrical, electronic or hydraulic and that wasn't currently bolted to an airframe. But I digress.

The reason for the high level of security clearance that kept me stuck at Halton for those two months became obvious when I arrived at Scampton and was promptly assigned to work in the top secret Blue Steel maintenance hangar.

Initially I was tasked with building a test rig that simulated all of the Blue Steel systems, which would facilitate the testing of the missile's electrical and electronic modules. The idea was to be able to simply plug the various modules into the test rig and then monitor the inputs and outputs from each module. Wherever possible the module was coupled to measurement circuit of some kind that illuminated either a green or red light to provide an indication of the module's serviceability. Ironically, although I didn't know it at the time, the Brass had already decided to retire Blue Steel and so my gizmo was in use for a mere 18 months.

When I wasn't building gizmos, I was fixing all manner of strange stuff, including special Blue Steel transporters, fire engines, runway de-icers, Palouste starter carts and much more.

Speaking of Blue Steel transporters, one bleak winter's morning, at around 02.30 a.m., I returned to my billet after a night out, looking forward to climbing in between the sheets for a nice, comfortable and well deserved sleep. But it wasn't to be! Stepping foot on camp, I quickly discovered that the RAF Police had been searching high and low for me for over two hours, even going as far as broadcasting my name over the station Tannoy system. It transpired that the Snoops had been trying to locate me because a Blue Steel transporter, carrying one of the missiles, had broken down while negotiating a roundabout on the A1 and I was needed to go out there to get it going again. The transporter was travelling in an escorting convoy of several vehicles, including a fire engine, RAF police and civilian police. Because of the breakdown, the whole convoy had ground to a halt, resulting in a major congestion on the roundabout.

It took until about 5.30 a.m. to get the transporter ready to roll again, but then we were informed that the escorting fire engine had developed a problem that prevented the convoy from moving. By this time, both the RAF and civilian police were becoming increasingly concerned that the large convoy was blocking a major roundabout on the A1. In addition, the Blue Steel missile was parked on the side of the road just asking for some drunk driver to crash into it. Luckily we got everything moving by about 7am – just before the rush hour started in earnest.

Of course there was a subsequent enquiry, which resulted in a new Standard Operating Procedure that required electrical technicians to be on standby at strategic locations along the convoy route so that they could respond within 30 minutes

As has been mentioned already, elsewhere in this book, there were nearby 'ponds' of water into which anyone contaminated by HTP were to be immediately immersed. My recollection of these is that they were orange plastic baths full of water on which multiple ping-pong balls floated. Well, I've had the extreme displeasure of being tossed into one, fully clothed, when HTP splashed during a missile refuel on a transporter. Happy days!

***

Periodically, when Mickey Finn exercises were called by Bomber Command (later, Strike Command) the normally almost deserted, remote dispersals at distant airfields became instantly populated and hives of activity for a few days when aircrews, ground crews and other support personnel descended on them to fulfil the intent of the exercise. They used the ground equipment, MT vehicles and other equipment, which was there waiting for them, all ready to use. They also slept in the caravan sleeping accommodation and ate food from the on-site kitchens, making them almost completely independent of the host station and its facilities. I wonder if any of those infrequent sojourners ever wondered who maintained the vehicles and equipment and made sure the caravans were fully serviceable and ready for use? Well behind the scenes, each of the dispersals was staffed by two or three technicians who were responsible for keeping all of the above facilities in peak working condition and making sure that the vehicles and appropriate ground equipment were all fully fuelled. For a time, I was one of those technicians, spending three months at RAF Boscombe Down. Each technician was provided with a vehicle and took turns to be on standby and within VHF radio range of the station.

And then I got posted to Goose Bay!

***

Officially, Goose Bay in the Canadian province of Labrador, was a 12-month, unaccompanied tour and like Gan, a remote island in the Indian Ocean or Salalah in Oman at the bottom of the Arabian Peninsula it was considered by most as something of a punishment posting. My posting to Goose Bay came about very quickly and just happened to coincide with an interview during which my boss lectured me on the consequences for airmen who allowed themselves to become too closely involved with WRAF Officers. Apparently, living unobtrusively in a cold, damp, houseboat, moored on the River Witham in Lincoln, wasn't enough to keep our affair secret. Still she was beautiful and worth it.

Thus I arrived at Goose on the Christmas re-supply VC10, on 22nd December 1969. On board with me were the wives of approximately half of the married men at Goose (as it is nicknamed by those who serve there or visit). The women were going there to spend Christmas with their husbands because the men had to remain on duty and were therefore unable to go on home leave. We arrived in a total White-out and –35 Celsius. Visibility on the ramp was about 50 metres in snow and 35kt wind as we struggled to walk from the aircraft into No 1 Hangar, where I was to spend almost every waking moment for the next two and a half years.

Most of the wives had dressed up to the nines to meet their husbands, but their (1960s) ultra short mini skirts, white knee boots and silk blouses were no match for the driving snow and minus 35 degrees temperature. But they sure looked good.

The next day, half of the RAF detachment climbed aboard the VC10 to go home for Christmas. And then about an hour after they had left, I discovered that all my baggage was also on its way back to Brize Norton. Five weeks and some four or five aircraft from Brize Norton later, I eventually got my bags.

Although Goose is cold – a very dry cold – you can fall in the snow and not get wet because it doesn't stick to you, but neither can you make snowballs with it. The climate there is so dry that static electricity is a major problem and people have to walk around earthing themselves on every pipe or radiator they pass. Miss a few earthing opportunities and you are rewarded with a massive static electric shock when you touch something or someone.

My role at Goose was to take care of the maintenance and carry out the repairs on all of the ground equipment and vehicles (Houchin power trolleys, Palouste starter trolleys etc.) I was consequently involved in many hangar engine starts and other procedures. I wonder what the crew of one Vulcan thought when their starboard main wheel fell through the hangar floor just after both port side engines had started? Or what about the two crew chiefs who became distracted whilst refuelling and allowed their Vulcans to tip onto their tails by allowing fuel to flow into the rear tanks first? An expensive mistake!

Everything suffered from the cold, particularly things made of rubber. The 3 inch thick power cables on the Houchin would shatter into a million pieces if dropped after a couple of hours in the open. The oleo seals on all aircraft shrank, stiffened and in some instances cracked and fell to pieces. The Vulcans and Victors didn't suffer this as much as the Hercules aircraft. One Hercules pilot was so keen to get home, despite totally shattered oleo seals on his aircraft, that we ended up standing on its rear loading ramp and pouring hydraulic fluid into the reservoir while he taxied from the pan out to the runway – with 90% of the fluid pouring out of the wrecked oleo seals. When he was lined up on the runway with engines at full power and ready to release the brakes, his crew chief threw us out and off he went. Try as we might, we never found out how he landed back at Lyneham, but I presume it was very gently. Meanwhile, we had to clean up all the spilt hydraulic fluid.

Goose had an annual carnival that was well known throughout the Air Force. We would have up to 20 Vulcans, Victors, Hercules and VC10s, all supposedly stranded at Goose during the Carnival. The festivities lasted for a straight seven day period during which no one did any work; instead, everyone participated in crazy competitions and of course, drank and drank and then drank some more. All of the teams were focused on one or another of the several drinking clubs on the airbase or in the local community. Although there was an RAF Officers and Sergeants mess, their combined membership amounted to just 15 individuals. Therefore the Junior Ranks Bulldog Club became the focus for most RAF goings on. Each drinking club sold plastic walking canes especially for the carnival. The hollow canes were approximately 3 ft long and 1.5 inches in diameter complete with a screw top. They were used to carry one's personal supply of booze as you went from event to event. As far as I remember, the capacity of a cane was approximately one bottle of spirits; just unscrew the top and have swig as and when necessary.

Most of the events were highly amusing and some even tested Cockpit Resource Management to the full – e.g. strapping 5 or 10 aircrew onto a single pair of 20ft long 'skis' – or strapping two pilots onto one pair of snow shoes. Can you imagine starting out to build a life size ice sculpture of a sperm whale if you were sober? (60ft long 30ft tall at the flute and with six Eskimo hunters in kayaks). Or dressing up as an Egyptian slave, wearing nothing more than flip flops, a loin cloth and fake tan cream and then prancing around an ice rink at –15-20 Celsius for over an hour. But it was fun. At least the bits I remember were fun.

The Bulldog club was officially the RAF Junior Ranks club, but it was popular with all ranks and with the local ladies. We held dances, discos and carnival events; several of us also played in local bands. Airmen could take turns to run the bar for a one-month period. During this time you were allowed to keep all the tips as well as all the profits from any extra events or services you were able to sell. In this respect, our relationship with the Vulcan crews was absolutely critical. The Vulcan panniers were always full of not just official spares, but also barrels of English Beer and delicacies such as Walls sausages, Danish Bacon, Cadbury's Chocolate and anything else the 'duty bar manager' thought he could turn a profit on. Fresh milk was also high on the list because cows couldn't survive the harsh climate, so we had to make do with re-constituted milk.

In addition to my main job I had a few secondary duties, including helping Eric Henry, our resident Physical Training Instructor, to teach arctic survival to the visiting aircrew, such as building snow-holes, igloos, tree shelters, trapping and ice fishing. I also had the dubious task of driving out onto the frozen lake to drill holes and measure the thickness of the ice. This was part of my standard duties and every week I was responsible for sending a signal back to Strike HQ reporting the ice thickness at certain points on the lake. Someone somewhere had calculated that if the runway became obstructed, a Vulcan could be diverted to land on the ice. Rather him than me, though.

I also had to maintain the electrical generators and radios at three 'Resource and Initiative' training camps owned by the RCAF and located on lakes in the wilderness, approximately 60 nautical miles east of Goose. In reality, these were fishing and hunting camps where senior officers used to go for a week or more of relaxation, hunting and fishing, courtesy of the Canadian taxpayer.

If you were someone who visited Goose back in those days, you would probably have seen two or three civilian light aircraft nestling like chicks under the wings of a Vulcan. These were owned by the Goose Bay Flying Club which, as a token payment for its hangar space, awarded a free flying scholarship each year to one member of the Detachment. I was fortunate to win this in 1970 and our Squadron Leader Ops (who moonlighted as CFI) taught me to fly. His name was Tony Ingoldby, a tall slim guy and a former Red Arrow pilot. In those days, however, I just called him Sir because, even though discipline at Goose was relaxed, 'other ranks' and Squadron Leaders were still not on first name terms. In later years, I tracked him down to his retirement home near RAF Scampton. Sadly he had passed away just a couple of months beforehand, but I was able to speak to his widow. Thanks to him I got my Canadian PPL and for the next 2 years enjoyed some of the most enjoyable flying anywhere in the world – flying on wheels, on skis, on floats and amphibious floats. There was a never ending stream of people wanting to fly. When my colleagues went off on fishing & hunting trips, I would fly out to them and 'air-drop' essential supplies that were too heavy to carry, particularly the beer. In doing so, I managed to build relationships and fly with a couple of the small 'Bush Airlines' operating from Goose and also got to fly to remote Inuit settlements including North West River, Churchill Falls, Cartwright, Kujjiaq and Frobisher Bay.

I'm not 100% sure, but I think I may have been the first and perhaps the only AOC's Pilot with the rank of Junior Technician when I took Air Vice Marshal Sir Dennis Spotswood, Air Officer Commanding Strike Command, on an aerial sightseeing tour of the Goose Bay area whilst he was there for an AOC's Inspection. Certainly the RAF News made a big splash about it. His wife (or more accurately, her enormous fur coat) almost caused me to crash the aircraft, but that is a story for another time.

Overall Goose was just brilliant. I extended my tour three times before the RAF eventually frog-marched me onto a VC10 and back to the UK. We had probably the highest divorce and buy-out rate in the RAF because so many guys fell in love with the place, the local ladies or just the Canadian way of life and simply stayed there, often abandoning wives and family back in the UK. As for me; I owned a car, a Skidoo snowmobile and played drums in a band with a bunch of USAF guys – and did a lot of really great flying.

Postscript: In July 2015 I was fortunate to be able to make my first return visit to Goose since leaving in 1972. Luckily, I was able to do it at the controls of a light aircraft that a friend and I flew across the Atlantic. I was therefore able to fly around to see how much Goose had changed in the intervening years. Gone were the 8000 USAF and RCAF staffs and their families, replaced by approximately 3000 fairly rough and ready construction workers building a new Hydro Electric Dam at Muskrat Falls about 3 miles from Goose Bay (the third Hydro Electric Dam on the Churchill River). There is now just one restaurant in Happy Valley and the Hudson's Bay Store has closed down.

I made contact with a couple of former RAF Goose Bay staff, who resigned and still live and work at Goose. They very kindly arranged for us to get into the 'Air Forces Museum', which unfortunately is still located within the USAF restricted area. In the museum, we came across a photo on display that I didn't know existed. It shows a much younger version of me (kneeling) and Mick Wilkes, both of us engaged in carving the ice sculpture of the Sperm Whale (mentioned earlier). If you look carefully, you can still see my nickname 'Squiffy' written on my mittens.

As a final note, I was invited to do a one-hour live interview on CBC (the Canadian Broadcasting Corporation) describing just how much Goose had changed in the 40 years since I had been there. I found it difficult to describe the changes without sounding too negative and had to forcibly remind myself that my memories were those of a naïve and impressionable 19 year old, whose 'life experiences' had quite literally 'exploded' upon arriving at Goose Bay and that I was now looking at Goose through much older, and far more cynical eyes.

Creating the Sperm Whale ice sculpture

Acknowledgements

Although the genesis of this book is a recollection of my personal memories, it owes much of its content to the input and support of friends, former colleagues and others.

Geoff Supple has been my main collaborator in this endeavour. It's hard to know where to begin to thank him but I'll start with the many discussions we have had over the years of our experiences on the Line at Waddington. Then, for the articles he has written, that he allowed me to incorporate in this book and for his many emails with comments on my drafts that he kindly read, frequently filling in gaps in my often faulty memory and adding other stories of incidents that he remembered. Finally, for the photographs from his personal collection and those provide by George Chinnery that he passed along to me.

My heartfelt gratitude to Dorothy Eilbeck, my friend of many years, for taking on the Herculean job of editing the entire book and for tackling my addiction to the overuse of commas. My thanks also for her contribution of an RAF wife's view of life at Waddington.

I wish to acknowledge and thank artist Derek Blois for allowing me to use his beautiful painting of 'Night Vulcan' which graces the front cover. I first saw a copy of this painting that Derek posted on the *Facebook* page, '*Vulcans, Victors and Valiants*'. It took me back to night shift on The Line, reminding me of how a Vulcan looked sitting on a dispersal pan on a wet winter night when pre-flights were complete and it was locked up, ready for the next day's sorties. To me, the picture also manages to convey the air of beautiful but deadly menace that the Vulcan seemed to embody. Derek is a prolific artist who has many amazing paintings, aviation related and otherwise, that can be viewed on his website http://www.derekblois.co.uk from which prints can be purchased at a reasonable price.

Thanks also to former Line colleague and friend George 'Mitch' Mitchell for his two stories, but also my grateful thanks for sending me a copy of the Vulcan B1A Servicing Manual (AP101B-1901-1A) that proved invaluable for confirming technical details and which gave me access to the Vulcan related diagrams included in this book that I was able to use after a little Photoshop 'massaging'.

My thanks to Tom McCormick who gave me permission to include two of his posts on the Pprune website thread, 'Did You Fly the Vulcan??' which I combined to form Bonus Chapter 2. (www.pprune.org/aviation-history-nostalgia/111797-did-you-fly-vulcan-merged.html).

Thank you also to Eric Bickley-Faux for sending me several great Vulcan photographs from his father's collection and to George Chinnery for the photos of the lads of Flight Line Squadron taken during those long ago days.

My final thank you is to my long-suffering wife Pam who has put up with me being physically present but mentally AWOL while I was writing and putting this book together.

In Memoriam

Much water has flowed under the bridge since those far-off Cold War days and in the intervening years some of the Line Squadron men named in this book are no longer with us. I take this opportunity to honour their memories.

Stan Eilbeck

Stan joined the RAF as an Apprentice in 1958 at the age 16 and trained as an Electrical Fitter (Air) at RAF Halton. He was posted to RAF Waddington in 1961 with the rank of Junior Technician when he graduated from his apprenticeship. Except for a 1-year unaccompanied tour to RAF Labuan, Borneo during the 'Indonesian Confrontation', he spent his entire RAF career at Waddington, eventually achieving the rank of sergeant and an HNC in Electrical Engineering. On completion of his RAF service in 1972, he accepted a position with British Aerospace at Warton near Preston in Lancashire.

Stan began his civilian career at British Aerospace as an Electrical Systems Design Engineer in the Electrical Systems Department, progressing to the Electronics Department and the Avionics Systems Engineering Department. He ultimately became a Systems Engineering functional specialist, supporting all Military Aircraft projects and made a significant contribution to many projects, including the Tornado, Typhoon and Nimrod.

In the later years of his career, Stan was recognized for his work in developing some of the processes and procedures required to certify complex electronic components and safety critical systems. His technical knowledge was complemented by his ability to work with people: listening, encouraging and using his own style of Cumbrian pragmatism to reach solutions that were innovative whilst being highly practical.

Stan retired in 1999 as a senior executive and had 18 years of happy and productive retired life. His many interests included painting, fell walking, running, gardening, fishing and cooking.

Sadly, Stan passed away on August 31, 2017 and is sorely missed by his beloved wife Dorothy, their children and grandchildren.

Stephen John 'Johnny' Thorne

Johnny Thorne was born in 1943 and trained as an Air Radio Fitter at RAF Locking. He was posted to RAF Waddington with the rank of Junior Technician on completion of training and worked on the Flight Line Squadron.

In the late 1960s, having reached the rank of sergeant, Johnny applied for and was accepted for aircrew training. At first, he served on Shackletons of Coastal Command but eventually became an AEO on the Nimrod, attaining the rank of Master AEO, equivalent to the rank of Warrant Officer and the highest non-commissioned rank in the RAF.

On retiring from the service in 1984, Johnny worked for a time teaching on RAF related topics in London before joining British Aerospace at Manchester, test flying the new version of the Nimrod. When the government scrapped the Nimrod in favour of the American AWAC, his job became redundant. Johnny then took up the position of Marketing Manager for America with the English Electric Valve Company in Lincoln. He held this position for a considerable time but eventually accepted the offer of a better position with Litton Industries, also as a Marketing Manager. Retiring from this work at the age of 59, he and his wife Carol founded a catering business 'Working Lunch Company' that delivered lunches to various educational establishments.

Sadly, Johnny passed away on August 11, 2009 at the age of 66. His interest and relationship with aircraft never left him, so in addition to his other work, he became a volunteer guide at Newark Air Museum, especially guiding visitors around the Shackleton; one in which he had actually flown in as a crew member. His ashes were placed there at the Shackleton and a garden bench was donated to the museum in his name.

Barry Goodall

Barry Price Goodall passed away on 25 June, 2018 at the end of a lengthy period of deteriorating health. He was 76 years old. He entered the service as a Boy Entrant, and trained as an Electrical Mechanic (Air) at RAF St Athan, South Wales.

Although Barry was a humble Senior Aircraftsman (SAC) he knew his way around the Vulcan and was always happy to unselfishly pass his knowledge on to newcomers to the ranks of the Flight Line Squadron. One of his favourite activities was driving the squadron vehicles thus earning him the nickname 'Clutch' by which Mitch Mitchell referred to him earlier, in chapter 10.

Barry fitted the profile of one of those people generally referred to as a 'free spirit'. Strangely, although he loved driving, he did not possess a civilian driving licence, although he did have an RAF Class 'C' licence which permitted him to drive only within the confines of an RAF station. Yet, I know of one instance when he drove a RAF Land Rover into the heart of the city of Lincoln. When giving a eulogy at Barry's funeral, Geoff Supple related the following anecdote that illustrates our colleague's helpful but cavalier attitude to rules and regulations.

One November evening the pair decided to go to Grantham for a night out. The fog was horrendous and the bus didn't turn up. Undaunted they tried to get a lift and were picked up by a man travelling along at a snail's pace, peering through the gloom to gingerly find his way. He was a Stonemason who had been working on Lincoln Cathedral and was returning to his home in London for the week-end. He didn't know the road and seemed to be very timid in the weather conditions. Barry, in his imitable way asked the guy if he wanted him to drive. The beleaguered Stonemason jumped at the chance to change seats, and so with Barry driving and Geoff hanging out of the window telling him where the verge was in relation to the car, they made it to Grantham in double quick time, despite the fog. The Stonemason was grateful when they reached the A1 with the car pointing in the direction London and where they parted company him. Perhaps the Stonemason might not have been quite so happy had he known that Barry didn't even have a driving licence!

His funeral notice stated; Barry passed away peacefully with the biggest beautiful smile on his face in such a relaxed manner, and is now at peace without any pain and suffering. Barry was a hard working incredible man who liked to laugh and have fun and had a tremendous love and passion for animals. Barry is survived by his beloved daughters Trudi and Helen and his former wife Beryl.

Dick Lowther

Based on information posted on the RAF Boy Entrants Association website, Dick Lowther, who was the airman trapped in the Power Compartment, as related in chapter 11, passed away circa 2004. No other details are available.

Geoff Sykes

After leaving the RAF, Geoff started a TV and radio repair business in the Lincoln area, but he also enjoyed several other pursuits. He was a rock climber in his younger life and a competitive cyclist all his life. He also enjoyed motorcycling and once found an old British motorcycle on a trip he made to India. Much to the horror of his family, he rode it all the way back to Lincoln, passing through some dangerous war-torn countries on the way. But it wasn't all outdoors that interested Geoff; he was also an active Chorister and singer with the 'Over the Hill Band'.

On the business side, having just bought a state-of-the-art video editing suite in the 1980s, he entered a contract with MoD to use it in the filming of an in-flight Vulcan-to-Vulcan refuelling operation over the North Sea. He then spent many happy hours flying alongside the Vulcans, filming the in-flight fuel transfer operation. However, MoD lost interest in the project, so Geoff was gifted the only historic film of the North Sea in-flight refuelling exercise.

Geoff passed away at St. Barnabas Hospice, Lincoln in September 2018 after losing his long battle with stomach cancer.

About Geoff Supple

When a vacancy for a trainee *Rock n Roll Legend* failed to appear on the Board at his local Jobcentre, Geoff decided to take the Queen's Shilling and join the Royal Air Force as an Aircraft Apprentice.

Born into a military family in 1943 he had already experienced Troopships, Travel, Sun, Sea and Sand. So, by the time he left home at 15 he had attended 8 schools round the World and was undaunted about his Apprenticeship at No. 1 School of Technical Training, Royal Air Force Halton as an Electrical Fitter (Air) in the 92nd Entry.

His first posting in 1962 was to 101 Squadron R.A.F. Waddington in Lincolnshire to work on the mighty Vulcan Bomber. He spent a total of 10 years maintaining the Vulcan including 1st and 2nd Line Servicing of the aircraft and Special (Nuclear) Weapons and Systems roles; numerous detachments and a 3-year family posting to R.A.F. Akrotiri in Cyprus.

Before completing his service and by now a Sergeant he enjoyed a short posting to the Oxford University Air Squadron at R.A.F. Bicester from where they operated 3 Chipmunk Training Aircraft.

By 1973 the *Rock n Roll Legend* train had long since left the station and he was too old to join the Circus so, with the princely sum of £305 in his pocket and a one-way railway ticket for himself and family he bade farewell to Military life.

College and a new career beckoned. He settled in the East Midlands and joined the Power Industry as an Electrical Engineer. He spent 30 years with them before retiring at 60 as a Telecommunications Engineer with the National Grid Company.

Geoff is married with a grown-up family, numerous Grandchildren and two Great Grandchildren. Since retiring he has enjoyed Volunteering in India Nepal and Sri Lanka. He has retained his interest in the Vulcan and is a volunteer and guide with Vulcan to the

Sky Project and has also helped at the International Bomber Command Centre in Lincoln.

Now that he is old and grey his Marathon Running, Skiing and Sailing have given way to the more leisurely pursuits of Travel, Cycling, Long Distance Walking and learning to play the Ukulele.

Like many old stagers Geoff is the eternal optimist and still dreams that one day a COLD WAR CAMPAIGN MEDAL will drop through his letterbox!

Geoff Supple with Vulcan XH558 for which he is a volunteer guide.

About the Author

A native of Coleraine, Northern Ireland, Brian Carlin joined the Royal Air Force as a Boy Entrant in 1956 to train as an aircraft electrician, four months prior to his sixteenth birthday. On graduating in 1958, he was posted to the Royal Air Force College Cranwell where he worked with Vampires, Meteors, Jet Provosts and Chipmunks, mostly on the flight line.

In April 1962, Brian was selected to participate in RAF's trials of the American made Skybolt air-launched ballistic missile at the USAF Eglin Air Force Base in Florida, but the Skybolt was cancelled before his departure for Eglin. Instead, he was posted to Bomber Command station RAF Waddington in March 1963 and internally posted to Flight Line Squadron, working with Vulcan Mk B1A aircraft. In June 1964, shortly after marrying his wife Pam, he was posted to RAF West Raynham, Norfolk to participate in the evaluation of the P1127 STOL Fighter in the Kestrel Tripartite Evaluation Squadron.

At the conclusion of the Kestrel Evaluation Trials in early 1966, Brian was posted to RAF Scampton and the Vulcan Mk B2, but later that same year, was posted to the Far East Air Force (FEAF). His wife Pam joined him three months later. Most of Brian's service in FEAF was in the Electrical Servicing Bay at RAF Changi, Singapore.

Repatriated to the UK in August 1968, with a posting back to RAF Scampton, he served out the remainder of his time in the RAF, attaining the rank of Sergeant before entering civilian life in February 1971.

Working in the Industrial Gas Turbine industry initially as an Electrical Draughtsman, he was promoted to Engineer status after obtaining an HNC in Electrical Engineering. Working for several years in the UK, he eventually accepted a transfer to the United States, initially to Houston, Texas and then later to San Diego, California where he retired in the year 2000 having risen to the position of Principal Project Manager.

Brian has continued to live in San Diego with his wife Pam and near his two daughters and five grandchildren. He helps one of his daughters to manage a small staffing agency and writes articles and books as a hobby.

Brian Carlin and Geoff Supple on board the USS Midway Museum - a decomissioned aircraft carrier permanently docked in San Diego bay, California.

CPSIA information can be obtained
at www.ICGtesting.com
Printed in the USA
LVHW091046190521
687767LV00012B/246